THE HISTORY OF
THE RUGBY WORLD CUP

First published in 2015
by Murray Books (Australia)
www.murraybooks.com
This edition published in 2019

Copyright © 2015 Murray Books (Australia)
Copyright © 2015 Peter Murray
Licensed to G2 Entertainment UK

ISBN: 978-1-78281-490-0

Compiled by Peter Murray and Lorri Lynn

Images: Shutterstock, Getty Images

The author and publisher have made every effort to ensure the information contained in this book was
correct at the time of going to press and accept no responsibility for any loss, injury or inconvenience
sustained by any person or organisation using this book. Some editorial may have been used from the
Public Domain.

CONTENTS

WORLD CUP HISTORY

1987

The inaugural, 1987 Rugby World Cup was hosted jointly by New Zealand and Australia, with New Zealand hosting the lion's share of matches. The tournament consisted of 24 pool-stage matches before proceeding to the quarter-final and semi-final rounds. Satellite television was still in its infancy at the time, so the viewing audience was limited to 300 million worldwide and spectator attendance of 604,500. This meant that the revenue earned by the host countries was far more limited than it is today, although New Zealand authorities announced that World Cup Rugby boosted the country's GDP.

With 16 places available, IRFB member nations filled the first seven spots. These nations were Wales, Scotland, New Zealand, Ireland, France, England and Australia - South Africa was excluded, due to the international sporting boycott in place as a result of Apartheid. As an inaugural tournament, the cup had no set precedent for qualification for the remaining nine places, so invitations were sent out instead. The final nine places were thus filled by Zimbabwe, USA, Tonga, Romania, Japan, Italy, Fiji, Canada and Argentina. Allegedly, Russia refused its invitation for political reasons, and Western Samoa, although a better team than other invitees, was puzzlingly omitted.

A four-pool system was adopted for the group stage, and each team played the three other members of their pool once to determine the top two teams in each pool. A basic points system was implemented to reward wins and draws only, and the two leading teams from each pool then advanced into the knock-out quarter-finals. Pool runners-up then played the winner of an opposing pool to determine the four teams who would play in the semi-finals. The two losing semi-finalists played each other for third place, while New Zealand and France battled it out for the Webb Ellis Cup. At the final whistle, it was New Zealand, the tournament's favourites, who emerged the outright, 29-9 victors.

1987 will be remembered as the year famous for the scoring imbalance between teams. It was no surprise that the seven IRFB members, with a strong rugby pedigree, were dominant throughout the tournament. In a sport generally used to seeing average winning scores sitting under 30 points, the inaugural cup was unusual in that many of the 24 initial pool games had the victors scoring over 40 points. Statisticians weren't surprised at the large gaps in the pool

games, with Fiji, Italy and Zimbabwe suffering the greatest loss margins, but Rugby Union was yet to advance beyond amateur status in many countries, and those who played in 1987 were pioneers for the game's ensuing growth 'back home'. To the credit of the less experienced invited nations, there were no world record losses recorded in 1987, but the All Black's Grant Fox managed a record-breaking 30 conversions for the tournament – a statistic that is yet to be beaten.

The final match saw 45,000 fans fill Auckland's Eden Park to see France take on the All Blacks. After a first half that saw New Zealand with a 9-0 lead, the French came out with all guns firing for the second half, but the host country fired back with forward power and accurate kicking. France gave it their all until the final whistle, with Didier Camberabero converting a try in the game's last kick, but the 29-9 score told the story – France had played themselves out in the semi-finals, and New Zealand had the stamina and skill to convincingly take the Web Ellis Cup.

The 1987 Rugby World Cup was lauded as an international sports success, and it became the catalyst for many nations becoming IRFB members, and for the continuing popularity of Rugby Union on a global level.

WORLD CUP HISTORY
1991

With the success of 1987 behind them, the IRFB found itself organising a tournament that far outstripped its predecessor. With world attention now focussed on the game, the cup was to be co-hosted by five member nations. Wales, Scotland, England, France and Ireland took up the baton to introduce World Cup Rugby to the northern hemisphere, with England winning the bid to host the final game at Twickenham Stadium in London.

In all, 33 nations vied for a place in the 1991 Rugby World Cup, which inspired the IRFB to adopt a new strategy. From the outset, the qualification system changed, although the number of teams to play for the cup remained at 16. The IRFB automatically accepted the eight 1987 quarter-finalists, who were not required to take part in qualifying matches. With the original invitation method discarded, 25 nations then took part in a qualifying process that determined the eight remaining spots in the tournament. Interestingly, the 1991 line-up had only one change from that of 1987 –Western Samoa qualified, and Tonga was unsuccessful. The pool system remained unchanged, as did the allocation of win, loss and draw points. The progression method of teams to the quarter and semi-finals was also identical, as was the play-off for third and fourth places.

In the four years between tournaments, Rugby Union had grown in popularity on a worldwide level, and the result was a far closer competition in the pool stage. Early shocks came when Wales finished third in their pool and were eliminated, along with Fiji, who lost all three of their games to France, Canada, and Romania. Most surprisingly, Canada qualified for the quarter-finals before falling to New Zealand, and newcomer Western Samoa also managed a quarter-final showing before losing to Scotland. As France fell to England, crowds experienced the thrill of the game at its best when Australia managed to beat Ireland in a nail-biting finish that sporting legends are made of. Ireland took the lead 18-15, when Australia's David Campese was outpaced and outclassed by Ireland's loose-forward, Gordon Hamilton. Hamilton virtually flew over half a pitch length to score a try that took the Wallabies by surprise, and it was only when Australia's Michael Lynagh managed a late try that rendered Ireland a point behind at the final whistle, and the spectators hoarse.

Two closely contested semi-finals, one played between England and Scotland in a typically Scottish downpour of rain in Edinburgh, and the other between Australia and New Zealand in Dublin, saw England and Australia advance to fight it out for the cup in the final at Twickenham Stadium in London watched by 1.75 billion viewers worldwide.

England had earned its place in the final by adopting a game thick with forward domination, but public criticism led by Australia's David Campese resulted in what appeared to be a tactical change of heart, which proved to be England's undoing. The only try of the match was scored by Australia's prop, Tony Daly, and a deliberate knock-on by the Wallabies resulted in a penalty, which England tried to argue should have been a penalty try. English protests, fuelled by 56,000 spectators, fell upon deaf ears, and the fate of the hosts was sealed - Australia won 12-6 in a match that was not one of Rugby Union's best, but more importantly, World Cup Rugby became a permanent fixture among the world's greatest sporting competitions.

WORLD CUP HISTORY
1995

It was fitting that the third Rugby World cup was hosted by South Africa. In 1992, the IRFB readmitted the Springboks to the competition once negotiations for the abolition of Apartheid were underway, and the game became global in every sense of the word from that point on. 1995 was also to be the last year of the cup with Rugby Union's amateur/professional status affecting who could play and who couldn't.

For the first time, the cup was to be hosted by one country alone, and the final was to be played at Ellis Park in Johannesburg. Again, 16 nations were to take part, with 32 games in all to determine the winner. 1991's eight quarter-finalists automatically entered the tournament, as did South Africa as the host country. The final seven nations were decided through the regional qualification process, and the final line-up consisted of Western Samoa, Wales, Tonga, South Africa, Scotland, Romania, New Zealand, Japan, Ivory Coast, Italy, Ireland, France England, Canada, Australia and Argentina. The points system in the pool phase was altered to accommodate 1 point for playing.

From the beginning, there was little doubt that the Springboks had what it took to reach the finals, and they managed an undefeated advance to the final game. New Zealand's incredible 145-17 win over Japan in the pool play-offs rattled more than a few record books, and both Canada and Ivory Coast scored the first no-scores in the tournament's history. In the quarter-finals, South Africa trounced Western Samoa, and France beat Ireland. England won its quarter-final against Australia by only three points, and New Zealand outplayed Scotland to advance.

The 1995 Rugby World Cup is also renowned as being the first time many international fans saw New Zealand's Jonah Lomu in action. When the enormous youngster bulldozed his way through Ireland, and chalked up four tries against England in the semi-finals, a superstar was born. Sadly for Ivory Coast's Max Brito, a serious injury only three minutes into the game against Tonga rendered a permanent quadriplegic.

The semi-final game between South Africa and France was very tightly contested and virtually underwater, with France losing by four points. New Zealand proved itself superior to England, who ultimately lost the match for third place against France. South Africa and New Zealand then battled it out in a

final match that had 2.67 billion viewers worldwide on the edges of their seats until after the full-time whistle. At half time, South Africa was in the lead, with the scores at 9-6, but the All Blacks responded with a drop-goal and tied the game. With no further points scored, the cup final was then forced into extra time, and took South Africa's Joel Stransky to score a drop-goal and give South Africa the cup.

Following South Africa's victory, New Zealand revealed that the entire team had suffered food poisoning less than 48 hours before kick off. Conspiracy theories about the source of the rogue meal continue to crop up, with the most popular being either the prawns or the water served by a mysterious waitress calling herself 'Suzie'.

Perhaps one of the greatest tributes paid to the ambassadorial role that sports can play, was made when Nelson Mandela presented the Web Ellis Cup to François Pienaar, South Africa's captain. Ellis Park in Johannesburg witnessed Pienaar and Mandela, the latter resplendent in Springbok's shirt and cap, celebrate so much more than a victory in world Rugby Union, and the symbolism of that day remains a high-point for sportspeople everywhere.

WORLD CUP HISTORY

1999

The fourth Rugby World Cup heralded a number of changes to the tournament, brought about by the game's increasing popularity and the number of nations vying for a place in the international sporting arena. The first of the 'professional' cups was hosted by Wales, with England, France, Ireland and Scotland providing the majority of match venues.

The most significant change was that the tournament grew to accommodate 20 teams, in place of the 16 teams that had made up the three previous competitions. Only four teams were to automatically qualify – Wales (as the host), and the three winners from 1995 (South Africa, New Zealand and France). The final 16 places were to be fought out between 63 nations, and a last-chance repechage tournament was to be held as a means of selecting the last two teams from the runners-up in each of the qualifying zones. The final line-up for the last Rugby World Cup of the century consisted of Wales, United States, Uruguay, Tonga, Spain, South Africa, Scotland, Samoa, Romania, New Zealand, Namibia, Japan, Italy, Ireland, France, Fiji, England, Canada, Australia and Argentina.

At the new Millennium Stadium in Cardiff, which was partly funded by £126 million in British lottery takings, Wales triumphed 23-18 over Argentina in the tournament's first game. By the time the final whistle sounded the end to the tournament a month later, and as Queen Elizabeth II handed over the Webb Ellis Cup, 1.75 million spectators had witnessed Rugby Union's greatest contest in the flesh.

The pool system was expanded to include five pools of four teams, and the pools were distributed between England, France, Northern Ireland, the Republic of Ireland, Scotland and Wales. The points system remained unchanged from the two previous tournaments, but qualification for the quarter-finals became more complicated. Each of the five pool winners advanced to the quarter-finals, but the five pool runners-up, along with the best third-place winner across all pools, were to face each other in quarter-final play-offs. The three winners of those play-offs would then proceed to the quarter-finals, to face five teams who had earned a week off.

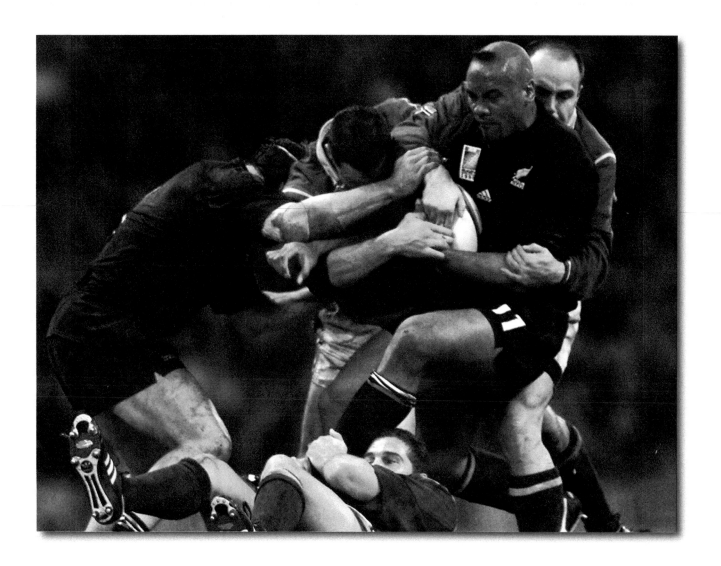

Apart from New Zealand's 110-3 pasting of Italy, the pool stage delivered no surprises, with New Zealand, Australia, South Africa, Wales and France advancing directly into the quarter-finals. England, Scotland, Ireland, Samoa and Fiji, as the pool runners-up, were joined by Argentina for the play-offs. England and Scotland beat Fiji and Samoa respectively, but it was Argentina, the competition's self-confessed amateurs, who caused the greatest upset by ousting Ireland in a 28-24 win on Irish soil.

Argentina, England, Scotland and Wales all went down in their quarter-finals, leaving Australia to beat South Africa 27-21 in extra time in their semi-final. It was however, the France – New Zealand semi-final that garnered most attention, as France managed to turn a half-time, 10-24 shortfall into a full-time 43-31 win and advance to their second Rugby World Cup final.

The Millennium Stadium was filled to its 72,500 capacity, and with 3 billion viewers tuned in around the globe, Australia and France faced each other in what would be second finals for each team. In the first half, France attacked and Australia defended, with penalty kicking dominating play. At half-time, France found itself struggling after an injury-induced substitution and a penalisation, and Australia led 12-6. Well into the second half, France began to falter, and the Wallabies took full advantage of its goal kicking prowess to triumph 35-132 after time-on.

WORLD CUP HISTORY
2003

An early contractual dispute between RWC Limited and New Zealand Rugby Union resulted in Australia hosting all 48 of the 2003 Rugby World Cup's matches without its Pacific neighbour. Having hosted the Olympic Games only three years earlier, the reigning Rugby Union world champions were well placed to accommodate the 1.8 million spectators who ultimately arrived to cheer on their nations as they went into battle.

The eight quarter-finalists from 1999 were automatically included, and 81 teams vied for one of the 12 qualifying places in games that spanned five continents, with the process again including the repechage system to determine the last two berths. The final line-up was comprised of Wales, Uruguay, United States, Tonga, South Africa, Scotland, Samoa, Romania, New Zealand, Namibia, Japan, Italy, Ireland, Georgia, France, Fiji, England, Canada, Australia and Argentina. Several key players for Fiji, Samoa and Tonga, who played abroad for professional clubs, were forbidden to take part in representing their nations, much to the dismay of their respective countrymen.

The IRFB had been criticised for the over-complicated, knock-out system introduced in 1999, so it reverted instead to the earlier system of advancing the top two pool winners into the quarter-finals. A new bonus-point system was introduced into the pool play stage, and it awarded points for tries and small losses along with increased win-draw points.

Australia and Argentina faced each other for the tournament's first match at the Telstra Stadium in Sydney, with the Wallabies winning 24-8. Argentina was again brilliant against Ireland, only missing out on a quarter-final berth by a mere point. Samoa delivered some surprising moments against England at first, while Fiji and Italy proved that they had the potential to become serious contenders in future tournaments. Nevertheless, the winning margins in the pools began to exceed those of 1987, and the Australia-Namibia match set the current world record with a blistering 142-0 result in favour of the Wallabies.

South Africa was not at its best in 2003, falling 29-9 to New Zealand in the quarter-finals, but the remainder of the knock-out matches were strongly contested, delivering New Zealand to face Australia and France to face England in the semi-finals. Ultimately, Australia and England battled it out for the trophy, while New Zealand took third place from England with a 30-14 result.

The first half of the Australia-England final began with the Wallabies drawing first blood, but in a little over ten minutes, England's Jonny Wilkinson answered with a penalty goal, adding a second nine minutes later and a penalty eight minutes after that. Ten minutes after that, Jason Robinson scored a try and took England to lead 14-5 at half time. England failed impress in the second half, with Wilkinson struggling for drop-goals, and the game went into extra time at the final whistle, with the score tied 14-14. With the scores frustratingly tied at 17-17 it was England's Wilkinson who kicked the final drop goal, handing the Web Ellis Cup to a northern hemisphere team for the first time in world cup history.

With the English making up reasonable contingent of the 1.8 million spectators attending, and with 3.5 billion watching the final televised event, England celebrated its first Rugby World Cup win as only the English can. Upon their arrival home, the squad stepped into London's Heathrow to the sound of massed fans singing Swing Low, Sweet Chariot. A national celebration day was declared, and hundreds of thousands of singing English fans lined London's best thoroughfares to witness their heroes driven through London in open buses – on their way to meet the Queen at Buckingham Palace and the Prime Minister at Downing Street.

WORLD CUP HISTORY
2007

n 2007, the tournament headed back to the northern hemisphere, with France outbidding England for hosting rights. At one stage, the bidding process had stalled, with both countries proposing alternatives that fell outside of the tender documentation, but the IRFB eventually opted for France's alternative dates over England's more complex two-tier tournament with an altered qualifying process. With 48 matches shoe-horned into 44 days, Wales and Scotland took care of the spill-over by hosting 6 matches between them. The Web Ellis Cup's popularity had grown so much that by the time the tournament began, 2 million of the 2.4 million spectator tickets had already been pre-sold!

2003's eight quarter-finalists automatically qualified for a berth, leaving the remaining 12 places to be filled through the regional qualifying process – with the obligatory two repechage spots. 90 countries now vied for the right to compete, and the final line-up was comprised of Wales, United States. Tonga, South Africa, Scotland, Samoa, Romania, Portugal, New Zealand, Namibia, Japan, Italy, Ireland, Georgia, France, Fiji, England, Canada, Australia and Argentina. Portugal debuted in 2007, and Uruguay failed to qualify.

The pool system remained unchanged but for one alteration – the top three winners in each of the 2007 pools would automatically qualify for the 2011 Rugby World Cup. With the points and bonus points system reflecting that of 2003, and third place renamed "Bronze Medal", 70,312 spectators in France's Stade de France witnessed the miracle of Argentina. Not only did the South American country beat France 17-12, it also went on advance to the semi-finals unbeaten!

Wales and Ireland suffered elimination in the pool stage, with South Africa, England, Australia, Fiji, New Zealand, Scotland, Argentina and France playing the knock-out matches. England overcame Australia in a closely contested game, and France beat New Zealand by the same margin – the first time the All Blacks had missed the semi-finals. South Africa were too good for quarter-finals debutante, Fiji, and Argentina pulled off another heroic upset to beat Scotland by six points and continue on their amazing journey. France and Argentina then lost their semi-finals, with Argentina taking the Bronze Medal and inspiring millions of South Americans to follow the game.

The Webb Ellis Cup was played out between England and South Africa, with the Springboks the clear favourite - after England lost 36-0 against them in the pool stage. With England fighting to win the cup for two consecutive years, Jonny Wilkinson kicked off, and both teams continued kicking with little scoring. After ten minutes, the scores were tied 3-3, and with penalties and inaccurate kicking continuing to dominate, South Africa managed to score a penalty and take a 9-3 lead at half time.

The 2007 Rugby World Cup match is still remembered for the pitch invasion by the notorious Jimmy Jump, but the Spanish streaker failed to upset the status quo. It took another 42 minutes before the scores changed, with England's Wilkinson converting a penalty, but a penalty kick restored the Springbok's lead. With South Africa's Percy Montgomery colliding with a television camera in an attempt to avoid the advertising boards at one point, nothing could stop South Africa from taking the match 15-6.

Spanish streakers aside, the most excitement to be had in 2007 was in the pool stages, as it often is in RWC history. With 2.2 million spectators and a worldwide television audience of 4 billion, it was Argentina who stole the show for many. Having managed to battle their way through the cup since 1987, the former amateurs with a dubious toehold on international rugby came within a solitary win of playing in the world's ultimate Rugby Union match.

2011

The seventh Rugby World Cup was hosted by New Zealand, after winning the bid over Japan and South Africa. With the 2003 controversy behind them, New Zealand planned to increase the size and capacity of Eden Park and other stadia, although both Japan and South Africa already had the infrastructure in place or underway thanks to their FIFA involvement. Far from celebrating the win, New Zealand's media, retail unions and government traffic authorities turned on its RWC organisers, heaping fuel on the fire of doubt over the country's readiness to host another tournament. The organisers fired back, and although Christchurch was subsequently struck by a devastating earthquake in 2011, a change of venue for some of the pool matches and two quarter-finals remedied the situation and put the lid on the naysayers.

Initial speculation that the number of participators was to be reduced to 16 proved itself unfounded, and the 12 top-three pool winners from 2007 were automatically afforded berths. The Tri-Nations Series scheduled for 2011 was also trimmed to include six games, and rugby nations in the northern hemisphere followed suit with their regional competitions. Among the eight remaining teams who qualified for 2011, debutante Russia was the only new face in a line-up that consisted of Wales, United States, Tonga, South Africa, Scotland, Samoa, Russia, Romania, New Zealand, Namibia, Japan, Italy, Ireland, Georgia, France, Fiji, England, Canada, Australia and Argentina.

Apart from Wales' 66-0 drubbing of Fiji and South Africa's 87-0 win over Namibia in the pool stage, the over all margins seemed less pronounced than they had in some earlier years. With Argentina's success in 2007 still fresh in the mind of many, the South Americans again impressed and made it into the quarter-finals before falling 33-10 to New Zealand. Australia knocked South Africa out to fall to New Zealand in the semi-finals and take the Bronze Medal from Wales in a tight match. France bested England and Wales won comfortably against Ireland, before France took Wales by a point in the semi-finals.

Fittingly held at Ellis Park, the venue of the inaugural Webb Ellis Cup final in 1987, France and New Zealand again faced each other for the ultimate prize. With two pool losses under France's belt, (and problematic relationship with their coach that was only revealed later), New Zealand were the clear

favourites. For reasons of geography, the spectator audience was lower than in previous finals, but billions watched worldwide as the French team answered the All Black's haka with a silent stare-down, followed by a creeping advancement in v-formation and an incursion over the half-way line to form a wall of bodies. Ultimately fined by the IRB for stepping over the line, the French nevertheless counted it as psychological one-upmanship prior to the game commencing.

France was forced into playing a defensive game from the outset, and with refereeing that was later denounced as 'shameful', New Zealand scored an early try. In the second half of the low scoring game, France fought back, answering a successful All Black penalty kick with a try, and converting it to reduce New Zealand's winning margin to a single point. The host nation however, was too good for the French, and as the game continued scoreless at 8-7, it was New Zealand's tackling and a penalty kick by Stephen Donald that won them the lowest scoring Rugby World Cup final in history.

WORLD CUP HISTORY

2015

The eighth Rugby World Cup tournament was played in 2015. The quadrennial Rugby Union World Cup was hosted by England. The tournament started on the 18 September 2015 lasting for 44 days with the final being played on the 31 October 2015. There was only one change to the lineup which had Uruguay replacing Russia with no new teams added to the tour-nament. This would be the first time the competition had no new team entrants.

New Zealand defended their 2011 title against Australia in the Final to take home their third consecutive Rugby World Cup with a 34 -17 win. Making New Zealand the first team in the tournament's history to win three consecutive titles in a row. South Africa took third place in the tournament after beating Argentina 24 – 13. No Northern Hemisphere teams got past the quarter-finals the first time in the competition's history.

The 2015 tournament drew a lot of media hype to it right from the start when Japan played against favored South Africa in the opening weekend. This much-contested match has come to be known as one of the "biggest upsets" in rugby's history. Japan brought home the win-ning try during extra time beating South Africa 32 - 34. England was defeated by Wales and Aus-tralia at the pool stage to become the only solo host team in the tournament's history not to make it through this stage.

The pool stage (first round) of the tournament had the 20 teams divided into 4 pools. This followed the same format used in the previous three competitions (2003, 2007 and 2011). The teams in each pool played one match against each other (ten games in a single round robin). Points were awarded for a win (4), draw (2) and one (1) bonus point for 4 tries or a loss of fewer than 8 points.

The 2015 World Cup Final had New Zealand become the first team in the history of the competition to retain their title for three years in a row. Making this game the perfect send-off as five of the All Blacks top players played their final World Cup game of their careers. Even as Australia turned up the heat during this exhilarating final Dan Carter managed to

The All Blacks scored 3 tries thanks to Ma'a Nonu, Nehe Milner-Skudder and Beauden Barret. Whilst the Wallabies were not far behind them scoring 2 tries from Tevita Kuridrani and David Pocock. Ben Smith became the first player to get a yellow card in a decider for tip-tackling of Australia's Drew Mitchell.

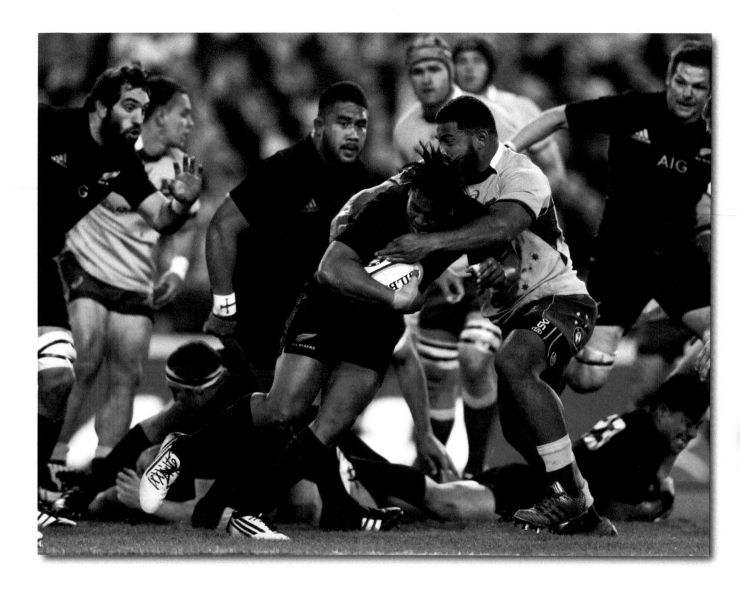

With Smith in the penalty box, the Wallabies came back in full force. They managed to bring the score to a close 21 – 17 in the final 15 minutes of the game by scoring 2 converted tries.

But New Zealand was not going to let Australia keep their score when Dan Carter in-creased the lead in the 70th minute of the game to 24 – 17. His long distant drop goal sailed through the goal posts to the roar of the crowd and sigh of relief to his teammates. After which he went on to kick a few more goals to help win New Zealand their third consecutive World Cup with a 34 – 17 victory over Australia.

The Australians put in a great effort but New Zealand all but dominated the field and pos-session. The 2015 Rugby World Cup saw quite a few firsts in the competition's history including that of the highest scoring final game.

Dan Carter was named the man of the match for his phenomenal gameplay and 19 points he scored. Points that included his remarkable long-distance drop goal kick that rounded off the teams lead in the match. A fitting end to his career with the All Blacks as heads off to play club rugby for Racing Metro a Parisian Rugby Club.

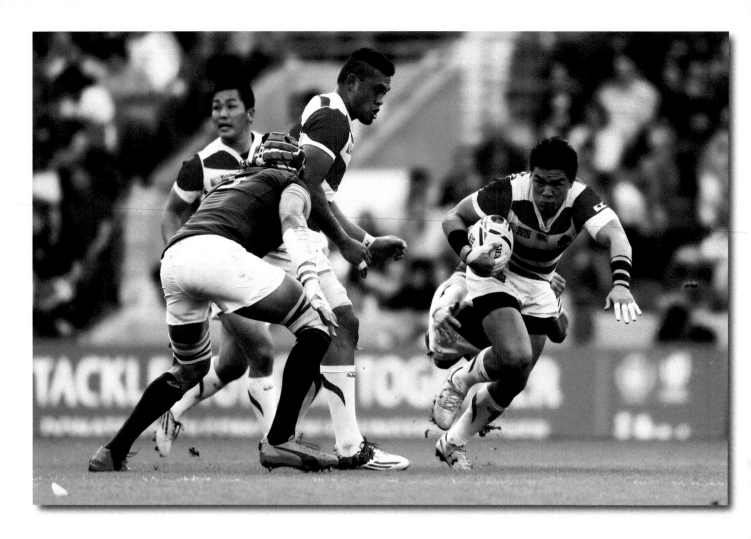

WORLD CUP HISTORY

MAJOR UPSET IN OPENING ROUND

The first round caused quite a stir when Japan went on to beat the favored South Africans leaving audiences around the world stunned. South Africa may have dominated territory and pos-session, but Japan made the most of their limited time in their opposition's half. Japan was unre-lenting when faced with their powerful Sprinbok opponents they were quick to find their rhythm. Led by scrum-half Fumiaki Tanaka who kept Japans game moving at a good pace and backed by the almost perfect kick of Goromaru.

Goromaru managed to bring the Brave Blossoms to 29 – 29 after converting his own try in the last ten minutes of the match. But the Springboks were determined to take back the game when replacement Handre Pollard managed to get them ahead with a penalty kick and eight minutes left on the clock.

As time went over the 80-minute game time and Japan not taking penalty kicks to even the score Hesketh pull out a winning left flank try after the ball was lobed across the field to him.

The ecstatic team did a victory lap of the field before taking a respectful bow giving thanks to their enthusiastic supporters.

The game found the Springboks most experienced Test side to be lacking in quite a few game play areas. In the first half of the opening game their kicking was below par, and indisci-pline caused them points in the second half. The game was a great disappointment for Springbok fans. Their game improved throughout the tournament as all pressure was on them to push their way through to next rounds. The match against Japan was an eye-opener for the somewhat com-placent Sprinboks. who still managed to survive the pool rounds to go through to the semi-finals ending the tournament in 3rd position!

WORLD CUP HISTORY

2015 RUGBY WORLD CUP QUARTER FINALS
SOUTH AFRICA VS WALES – 17 OCTOBER 2015 AT TWICKENHAM STADIUM, LONDON

This quarter-final was a close match with Wales having the lead by half time and manag-ing to regain it up until 75 minutes into the game. With five minutes to go Fourie du Preez found his opening and took off for the touch down that won the game for the Springboks defeating Wales 23 – 19.

Although both teams made a few errors they played an exhausting powerhouse of a match that was neck on neck. In the first 8 minutes South Africa took the lead with a penalty tak-en by Pollard and then again 3 minutes later putting the Boks in the lead with 6 points. But a few minutes later Wales managed to get into the game with a penalty taken by Biggar. After which the next few minutes of a truly intense first half saw South Africa and Wales battle it out. It was just before the half time whistle that Biggar's brilliant 30-meter drop-goal put Wales 1 point ahead.

The second half of this quarterfinal match had Wales once again taking the lead with an-other 3-point penalty score. But the Boks closed the gap with a drop-goal from Pollard who was on top form and after another penalty, 62 minutes into the match gave the Boks a 2-point lead. Wales turned up the heat with a counterruck that awarded them a penalty. Beggar's kick from wide right once had Wales take a 1-point lead at the 64-minute mark.

It looked like Wales might just get the game but du Preez saw an opportunity in the Wales blind side and took it to win the game for South Africa. South Africa would face New Zealand in the semi-finals.

Man of the match went to the Springboks flanker, veteran player Schalk Burger who proved his worth. Displaying old school tactics and barnstorming with his impressive ball-carrying and tackling. He has played in four Rugby World Cups and started in all seven of the 2015 World Cup Matches for the Springboks.

WORLD CUP HISTORY

2015 RUGBY WORLD CUP QUARTER FINALS
NEW ZEALAND VS FRANCE – 17 OCTOBER 2015 AT MILLENNIUM STADIUM, CARDIFF

New Zealand dealt a crushing blow to France in a 63 – 13 victory ensuring their place in the semi-finals.

A penalty had New Zealand score the first 3 points of the match six minutes in and Dan Carter kicked the ball effortlessly through the goal posts. But France soon leveled the scores with Spedding landing a penalty kick only 8 minutes in through the right-hand post. By halftime, New Zealand showed their dominance with a 29 – 13 lead over France.

The second half saw a bit of a punch up with McCaw sprawled on the field and being punched in the jaw by Picamoles who received a yellow card. The All Blacks kicked up their game even more as they rushed into a 41 – 13 lead with a try from Savea and conversion from Carter.

Coles was replaced by Mealamu 61 minutes into the game for the All Blacks with Du-moulin and Ben Arous being replaced by Debaty and Bastareaud for France. By this time France was already far behind the mighty All Blacks as they plowed forward on top form. By full-time New Zealand were far ahead of France having run them down and all but torn them apart.

France all but knew they were doomed after Savea scored the 300th World Cup Try for New Zealand. Throughout the game, the All Blacks had 51% Possession and 52% territory over the French. Making this their 9th win in a row over France who they beat by 1 point in the 2011 World Cup Final.

New Zealand moved on to the semi-final to play against South Africa after their victory over Wales. The Springboks have only beaten New Zealand twice out of their previous 12 matches.

WORLD CUP HISTORY

2015 RUGBY WORLD CUP QUARTER FINALS
IRELAND VS ARGENTINA – 18 OCTOBER 2015 AT MILLENNIUM STADIUM, CARDIFF

Ireland had their hopes of advancing to their first World Cup Semi-Final crushed when they lost 20 – 43 to Argentina.

The Irish team showed great strength of character despite being down by 5 of their key players due to injury. Only to lose Tommy Bowe to a knee injury during the game to be replaced by Luke Fitzgerald.

Within the first 3 minutes of the game Argentina's Moroni scored the game's opener and by the 13th minute of the match, the Puma's had a 17 – 0 lead over the Irish. By half time they were in the lead by 20 – 10, having had the scoring margin closed by an incredible try by Luke Fitzgerald.

Madigan's conversion and a magnificent try by Murphy 44 minutes in closed Argentina's lead to only 3 points. Ireland looked to be back in the game as they fought to keep their foothold and push forward but a penalty awarded to Argentina give them another 3 points. Unphased by this and more determined than ever the Irish are awarded another penalty was taken by Madigan to bring the score to Ireland 20 – Argentina 23.

The Irish were unable to score again as Argentina upped their game scoring with another two tries and two penalties to end the game with a 20 – 43 victory. Argentina moved to the semi-finals where they played Australia.

The man of the match for this exciting game was Nicola Sanchez who kicked 23 points for the Pumas during the game. This also made him the highest points scorer up to that point of the 2015 World Cup having scored 74 points.

Juan Imhoff became the first Argentinian in a Rugby World Cup to score 5 tries in a tournament.

WORLD CUP HISTORY

2015 RUGBY WORLD CUP QUARTER FINALS
AUSTRALIA VS SCOTLAND – 18 OCTOBER 2015 AT TWICKENHAM STADIUM, LONDON

Heartbreak for Scotland came in the form of a last-minute penalty kick by Foley winning the game for Australia by 1 point (Australia 35 – 34 Scotland). This was the closet quarter-final game of the tournament and the best game played by one of the six nations team during the 2015 World Cup.

Australia took the lead 9 minutes into the match with an exciting try by Ashley-Cooper. Scotland was soon to land a penalty by their captain Laidlaw and a try by Horne a couple of minutes later to take the lead from the Wallabies.

By half-time Australia had bounced back and Scotland lead by 1 point as the score reflected Australia 15 – 16 Scotland. The Wallabies took control in early in the second half with a try by Mitchell and great kick landed by Foley.

The Wallabies gained and kept control of the game by a very slim margin as Scotland made them work for each point. Until 74 minutes in with rain pouring down on them, Scotland got the ball and Slipper threw an intercept pass to Bennett who caught it and unopposed ran it under the posts for an amazing try. Scotland took the lead with a determination to keep the Australians from the semi-final.

With the game in the final minute, the ball was knocked on by Strauss and Australia was awarded a penalty. In the last 30 seconds of the game, the Scottish fans looked on holding their breath as Foley took the penalty kick. To the dismay of the Scots and elation of the Wallabies, Foley landed the kick as it sailed through the posts winning the game.

With Scotland out of the semi-finals for the first time in the history of the World Cup no Northern Hemisphere teams will compete in the semi-finals. Matt Giteau took the title of Man of the Match.

WORLD CUP HISTORY

2015 RUGBY WORLD CUP SEMI-FINALS
SOUTH AFRICA VS NEW ZEALAND – 24 OCTOBER 2015 AT TWICKENHAM STADIUM, LONDON

Clash of two great rivals in this semi-final saw New Zealand beat South Africa by a mere 2 points in a close match that had the fans gripping the edge of their seats. The reigning World Cup champions move on to defend their title in the finals with an 18 – 20 victory over the Springboks.

An epic match saw the Springboks take an early lead with a penalty kick from Pollard 3 minutes into the game. But New Zealand hit back when McCaw sent and over the top pass to Kaino who managed to brush pass a soft tackle to score a try in the first 6 minutes of the game. A clear conversion from Carter and the All Blacks pulled into a 4-point lead.

At the half time whistle, the Springboks had a 5-point lead over the All Blacks with a score of 12 – 7. Dan Carter literally kicked back 6 minutes into the second half with a dropkick that started to close the score gap. Until they eventually once again took the lead and held onto it.

South looked like they were starting to once again gain ground when Pollard kicked a penalty in the 58th minute but a few minutes later it was Dan Carters turn at a penalty kick taking the score to South Africa 15 – 20 New Zealand. Try as they might the Springboks could not take back the lead even after a great penalty kick from Lambie at the 69-minute match mark.

In the last few minutes, South Africa fought to get ahead but they could not manage to find a gap with the game ending with Matfield knocking the ball forward. There were a few New Zealand players that showed outstanding play during the match but Ma'a Nonu was the man who really deserved the honor. This semi-final match saw him have an all-time game-high with the second most meters (51) and 11 carries.

WORLD CUP HISTORY

2015 RUGBY WORLD CUP SEMI-FINALS
AUSTRALIA VS ARGENTINA – 25 OCTOBER 2015 AT TWICKENHAM STADIUM, LONDON

The Wallabies took control of the match and take a 13-point lead. Argentina fought back but was no match for the determined Australian team. The Wallabies battled on to a 15 – 29 vic-tory making it through to the finals and a facedown with reigning World Cup Champs.

As the starting whistle blew Hernandez took the starting kick and the game was off to a battling start with the Australians, Simmons, scoring the first try within 2 minutes. By half time it was clear that Wallabies were determined to get to the final and had a 15 – 29 lead over Argentina.

Argentina held on with Nicolas Sanchez kicking 5 flawless penalties and 54 minutes into the match they were trailing behind by only 7 points. The Wallabies gained even more ground as Drew Mitchell took a flat pass on the halfway then cut inside and headed for the posts. Three Argentinians rushed him with two more joining in as he reached the 22. A pass to Ashley-Cooper allowed the Australians to score another try and effortless conversion by Foley putting the Wallabies into a 15 – 29 lead with 8 minutes left of the game.

Adam Ashley-Cooper became the second player, after Jonah Lomu, to score a hat-trick in a semi-final of an RWC. Although Pocock's breakdown work makes him the player of the tournament, Adam's hat-trick is the play that the Australians are still talking about.

Argentina is to be commended on their 55% possession and 54% territory throughout the game-winning more scrums and lineouts than the Australians. But the Puma's were no match for the top form Wallabies.

The Australians advanced to the finals to play their Antipodean rivals to battle it out for the 2015 World Cup title.

THE INVINCIBLES

GRANT FOX
NEW ZEALAND

New Zealand's victory in the inaugural Rugby World Cup was due in no small part to Grant Fox's accurate kicking, which was no surprise, given that he was the All Black's leading goal kicker between 1985 and 1993. When the 1987 tournament began, Fox already had 8 conversions, 13 penalties, 3 drop-goals and a total of 64 points to his name for the All Blacks, and by the time New Zealand won the Webb Ellis cup on June 20, he had added another 30 conversions, 21 penalties, 1 drop-goal and 126 points to his international tally.

When Fox began his career as an All Black, his first international appearance was in a short tour of Fiji in 1984. At that point, he was still understudy to a number of key players, including Kieran Crowley, the All Blacks' top score kicker at the time. Fox was also forced to incur a ban in 1986, having joined the rebel Cavaliers' controversial tour of South Africa while the country was still under a sporting embargo as a result of Apartheid. Fox was not alone – all but two All Blacks players joined the rebel tour, and it was in that time that Fox's rugby prowess began to outstrip that of the man he understudied – Frano Botica. By the time selection for the Rugby World Cup XV was underway, there was little doubt that Grant Fox and his phenomenal scoring ability would be included.

Fox's contribution to the 1987 Rugby World Cup was a blistering one. In the pool stage, he scored eight conversions and two penalties against Italy, 10 conversions and two penalties against Fiji, adding two conversions and six penalties against Argentina. In the quarter-finals, Fox managed two conversions and six penalties in a lower scoring game that hose of the pool stage, and his seven conversions and a penalty against Wales saw the All Blacks' opponents fall in a 49-6 upset. Finally, at Eden Park in Auckland on June 20, 1987, Fox was the only multi-scoring All Black against France, taking four penalties and a drop goal, before his team took the inaugural Webb Ellis Cup.

From there, Fox's toured England, Ireland, Wales, France, Australia and Argentina over the next four years, and his scoring-rate was almost unbelievable, with test records falling like nine-pins in his path. Unlike many of his squad, Fox was never known for being a player of great flair or fleetness-of-foot, and some critics tagged him as *stodgy*, as a result of his inability to score a try. Nevertheless, Fox remained one of the most significant and effective players the All Blacks had seen, and until suffering an abdominal injury in 1991, the naysayers were quickly silenced.

After struggling to recover through the second Rugby World Cup, Fox finally found form again, and he played the 1992-93 season with his trademark scoring ability. Fox retired in 1993 aged 31, having played 46 tests and 32 games for the All Blacks, and notching up a stellar 1067 points, with one game as captain.

THE INVINCIBLES

JOHN KIRWAN

NEW ZEALAND

John Kirwan's role as a wing for New Zealand in the inaugural Rugby World Cup was without doubt a sensational one. At 22-years-old, Kirwan had already played over 20 international games for the All Blacks, and his inclusion in the Rugby World Cup side was never in doubt. His natural talent for the game, along with a maturity beyond his years, was complemented by determination, pace and a tall and broad stature unusual for a wing.

When the 1987 tournament kicked off, Kirwan already had 9 international tries and 36 points to his name, and by the time New Zealand won the Webb Ellis cup on June 20, he had added another 6 tries and 24 points to his international tally. Today, Kirwan ranks as the world's 18th highest try-scorer in Rugby Union test matches, with 63 caps and 35 tries for the All Blacks.

John Kirwan's rugby pedigree was evident in both sides of his family when he was recruited from Auckland Marist, a third-grade side, to play first-class Rugby Union at the age of 18. His grandfather, Jack Kirwan, was a Rugby League player for New Zealand, and his mother was from Otahuhu's renowned Hedge family. Kirwan's international career began in 1984, when he debuted against France at Christchurch. His first international try came a year later, against England.

Kirwan's contribution to the 1987 Rugby World Cup began with the first match. In a blistering game against Italy, he scored two tries (as did David Kirk and Craig Green) in a very one-sided game. With the All Blacks on fire, the ensuing game against Fiji netted Kirwan another try, and he scored again in the semi-finals, taking two tries in a whitewash of Wales. Finally, at Eden Park in Auckland on June 20, 1987, Kirwan scored the ultimate – a try in the inaugural Webb Ellis Cup grand final and victory for New Zealand.

From that moment in international rugby, Kirwan's path to sporting greatness was cast in stone. Although he was prone to back injury (as the result of an unprecedented growth spurt in his teens), Kirwan was infamous for his long field runs and try-scoring prowess. By 1992, he was the first All Black player to notch up 50 tests, and by time his first class career ended in 1994, he had a stellar 199 tries to his name.

After 1994, Kirwan played Rugby League for the Auckland Warriors until 1996, and was both player and coach for Japan's NEC Green Rockets and assistant coach for the Auckland Blues. A stint in Italy as their national Rugby Union coach preceded coaching Japan's national team, before returning home again and coaching the Blues in Super Rugby. In 2010, John Kirwan released the book *All Blacks Don't Cry: A Story of Hope*, which detailed his long battle with depression. He became involved in awareness campaigns dealing with depression and mental health, and was knighted for contribution to both mental health and rugby in 2012 – the year in which he was also inducted in to his country's *Sports Hall of Fame*.

THE INVINCIBLES

DAVID CAMPESE

AUSTRALIA

David Campese (AKA Campo) was voted Player of the Tournament for the 1991 Rugby World Cup, with an impressive six tries scored. With five years international experience under his belt, Campese came to the tournament with an impressive record, including having played in the Australian Under 21s as a teenage fullback without equal. Fast, accurate and unorthodox in his kicking action, Campese had played his first test match for Australia at the age of 19, and in 1991, he celebrated his 10th anniversary of international rugby by being instrumental in his squad's Webb Ellis Cup victory.

Campese's career as an international player of note began when he was selected, at age 19, for the Australian Under 21s when his outstanding talents were noticed by more than one rugby great at an infamous match against Fiji. Campese was instantly picked up for inclusion in the squad touring New Zealand in 1982, and although many were surprised at the selection, he soon proved himself with his outstanding talent and played his first test match for Australia at the age of 19. Soon, the unpredictable player who had the ability to tie the opposition in knots with unorthodox kicking and a stuttering step, became part of Australia's new-look *running squad*. Along with Nick Farr-Jones, Mark Ella and Michael Lynagh, Campese then rocketed to such prominence that he was colloquially known as the *Bradman of Rugby*.

As the Australian squad entered the 1991 tournament, they were coming off the back of a slump in form that had lasted since 1989, and Campese bore the brunt of a lot of criticism as a result of it. It was Barry John, the former Welsh rugby great who stood up for Campese and likened him to Pelé, in being *"associated with the very best and historic moments sport"*. Even Tony Ward, the Irish five-eighth, agreed, likening Campese to both Pelé and Maradona. Under captain Nick Farr-Jones, Campese sizzled, scoring tries against Wales and Argentina in the pool stage matches, and along with Michael Lynagh, starring in a quarter-final win over Ireland. It was in the semi-final against New Zealand that David Campese played possibly the greatest game of his career, pulling off a pass with trademark magician-ship and putting paid to his critics once and for all.

With New Zealand consigned to the third place play-offs, Australia faced England in the final, and Campese let the press know what he thought about England's playing style before the match. His comments were forthright but good natured taunts, aimed at the opposition's *boring* style of play. England changed its tactics for the final, and lost 12-6 to the Wallabies. Campese's cheeky, last word on the win was *"You know, if England actually played ten-man rugby, they probably would've beaten us."*

With an ultimate 64 tries in 101 Tests, Campese retired five years later, after a career of confounding many with his talent and offending others with his unapologetic opinions. His legacy today is that he was both the first of a generation of truly professional Rugby Union players, but also the last of the great risk-takers in a sport that has, like many, become more clinical in it evolution.

THE INVINCIBLES

JEAN-BAPTISTE LAFOND

FRANCE

Although France was unsuccessful in its bid to win the 1991 Rugby World Cup, Jean-Baptiste Lafond was the tournament's top try-scorer alongside Australia's David Campese. Lafond, a former CA Bordeaux-Bègles Gironde player, scored six tries – a phenomenal achievement given that France were eliminated by England in the quarter-finals. Under captain and French rugby hero, Serge Blanco, who would retire following France's quarter-final elimination, but not before Lafond sizzled at the peak of his career.

Lafond's international Rugby Union career began eight years earlier, in 1983, when he debuted as a wing for France against Australia. That match ended in a 15-15 draw, but from that point onward, Lafond's career took a giant leap forward. He played in the Five Nations Championship on numerous occasions, and by the time he retired in 1993, he had 36 caps and 101 points as a representative of his nation. In his last international game, France beat Wales – giving him a worthy send-off.

Drawn in Pool 4 for the preliminary stages of the 1991 tournament, Lafond scored a try against Romania, before taking another three tries against Fiji. In a closer match against Canada, he scored another try, and France advanced to the quarter finals. It was in the knockout game against England that Lafond scored the game's only try, with Thierry Lacroix the team's only other scorer with two penalties. Although Lafond and Campese drew with the highest number of tries scored in the tournament, Lafond advanced to the quarter-final stage with five under his belt, while Campese had three tries to his name at that point.

Lafond played international rugby for an additional two years before retiring. Following his retirement from international Rugby Union, Lafond has played for French clubs *Racing Club de France* and *Stade Français*.

THE INVINCIBLES

MICHAEL LYNAGH

AUSTRALIA

When Australia began on its victorious road to Rugby World Cup victory in October, 1991, Michael Lynagh had already been in sizzling form for a number of years. His debut as the Wallabies' number 12 had been made at a time when the great Mark Ella was the reigning number 10 fly-half for Australia, and Lynagh's impressive form in the shadow of the great Ella earned him a spot in the squad for the Wallabies' 1984 tour of Europe. By the time the whistle sounded for the first game of the 1991 tournament, Ella had retired, and Lynagh wore the number 10 jersey for his country – in only one of the four tests in Europe, he had scored an impressive two conversions and five penalty goals as inside-centre, and amassed Australia 21 of their final 37 points!

Lynagh began his career in an almost unorthodox manner, first as a star for his Brisbane school team, before spending his mid teens in the USA, where he played American Football. Returning to Australia, he immediately joined the Queensland University rugby team, where his talents rocketed him into first-class rugby and a spot on the State training squad. In 1982, upon leaving university, Michael Lynagh debuted for Queensland, and within the year, he had been selected for the Wallabies squad to tour France. Alongside scrum-half and captain, Nick Farr-Jones, Lynagh then honed his craft for 47 tests, culminating in the 1991 Rugby World Cup victory. When Farr-Jones retired two years later, there was no question that it would be Lynagh who would captain the squad, and he did so for the remaining two years of his international career.

Lynagh's spectacular role in the 1991 tournament began with three conversions and two penalties against Argentina in the first of Australia's pool stage matches. The next game against Western Samoa saw Lynagh as the only point-scorer for the victorious Wallabies, with three penalties, and in the final pool stage game against Wales he added another four conversions and two penalties to his tally. The quarter-finals gave Lynagh another feather in his cap, when he scored a try, as well as two conversions and a penalty, totally dominating a closely contested win against Ireland. A conversion and two penalties against the All Blacks in the semi-finals saw the Wallabies face England for the Webb Ellis Cup. In that match, Lynagh scored most points in a low-scoring face off – he took a conversion and two penalties over England's two-penalty final score and Tony Daly's single try of the match.

For the next four years of his international career, Lynagh went from strength, and he became one of Rugby Union's greatest ever fly-halfs, scoring a record-setting (at the time) 17 tries, 140 conversions, 177 penalties and nine drop-goals – with 60 test caps as a player and 12 as captain. Following his retirement in 1995, Lynagh went on to play for Englands *Saracens* for two years before becoming a sports analyst with Sky Sports UK. Michael Lynagh suffered a stroke in 2012, but he has largely recovered, suffering the partial loss of vision in both eyes. He holds an Order of Australia, and in 2001, Lynagh was inducted into the International Rugby Hall of Fame.

THE INVINCIBLES

ANDREW MEHRTENS

NEW ZEALAND

1995 was a ground-breaking year for South African rugby, and it was perhaps appropriate for Andrew Mehrtens to make his Rugby World Cup debut there for New Zealand. Having been born in South Africa to New Zealand parents, he spent the first four years of his life there before the family returned home to New Zealand. As part of the team whose loss to South Africa in the final of the tournament remains the most controversial issue in Rugby World Cup history, Mehrtens hit the ground running with three conversions from the outset –and he didn't stop!

Mehrtens' rugby career began as a junior player for Kaiapoi, but as a late developer, he only began to show promise in his late teens. The Mehrtens family already had a long rugby pedigree in New Zealand, with Andrew's father, Terry Mehrtens, having represented New Zealand against the Springboks and also played for Natal against the All Blacks in 1970. Andrew's grandfather, George Mehrtens, played internationally for the All Blacks in the 1920s. Having played internationally for the Under 19 squad, Mehrtens worked hard to prove himself in the three years leading up to the 1995 tournament, playing convincingly for Canterbury when it won the Ranfurly Shield in 1994. It was that performance that sealed Mehrten's fate as a future All Black, and he finally achieved his goal in a game against Canada, in which he scored a spectacular 28 points.

As the 1995 Rugby World Cup began, it soon became clear that the unstoppable combination of Mehrtens, Lomu and Kronfield was exactly what New Zealand needed to complete one of the best line-ups in its history. Mehrtens scored three conversions and four penalties in the All Blacks' first pool stage match against Ireland, and another two conversions, four penalties and a drop goal in the ensuing match against Wales. In the quarter-finals against Scotland, Mehrtens' tally blew out to add another six conversions and two penalties, and in the semis against England, yet another three conversion, a penalty and a drop goal! A much subdued All Blacks team faced South Africa in the host country's inaugural tournament appearance, the result of a mysterious bout of food poisoning that dropped the entire team only 48 hours previously. Only Mehrtens scored in a 15-12 defeat by the hosts, managing three penalties and a drop goal to lose by a single drop goal at the final whistle.

Mehrtens went on to represent New Zealand in an international career that lasted another nine years, and one that included him playing for the Harlequins in England (2005-2007) and Toulon (2007-2008), Racing Métro 92 (2008-2010) and Bézieres (from 2010) in France. In 2014, it was announced that Mehrtens had joined Australia's NSW Waratahs as their kicking coach.

Among his many achievements, Andrew Mehrtens is the second-highest All Blacks point scorer (857 points), he has kicked nine penalty goals on two occasions in a Test match, and holds the record for the most Test conversions – an astronomical 167. Mehrtens continues to remain a favourite with rugby fans, due mainly to his engaging personality and sharp wit.

THE INVINCIBLES

GAVIN HASTINGS

SCOTLAND

Gavin Hastings, known as *Big Gav*, is one of Scotland's most successful Rugby Union players. Having also captained Scotland in the Five Nations Championship and the British and Irish Lions in 1993, Hastings had been playing international rugby for nine years when he captained Scotland in what would be his final international appearance. His team's quarter-final loss to New Zealand was disappointing, but it did not take the shine from a career that was without doubt, one of the finest in the history of rugby in the British Isles.

Edinburgh born Hastings' first taste of rugby success was as captain of a Scottish schoolboy's side that was the first to win in England. He went on to captain Cambridge University in rugby in 1985, and also played for Auckland University in his sabbatical year in New Zealand. He also played for Watsonians and London Scottish, and he made his international debut for Scotland in 1986, taking his place alongside his brother Scott to kick 6 penalties in a winning match against France. Since that time, Scotland's favourite fullback has won 61 caps for Scotland (20 as captain) and 6 caps for the British and Irish Lions). He scored an impressive 733 points collectively for both sides, and was renowned for impressive rearguard actions and trademark, warrior-like fightbacks.

The first of the pool-stage matches saw Scotland facing the inexperienced Ivory Coast, and in an 89-0 victory, Hastings scored four tries, nine conversions and two penalties. Facing Tonga next, the team won 41-5, with both Scott and Gavin Hastings scoring a try apiece, and Gavin notching up a conversion and eight penalties. Going down 22-19 to France, Hastings nevertheless managed a very respectable conversion and four penalties, giving Scotland a quarter-final showdown against New Zealand. In that match, the Hastings boys starred, with Scott scoring two tries, and Gavin amassing three conversions and three penalties. Scotland lost 48-30, but it was no reflection upon the career of its captain.

Following his retirement from international rugby, Hastings joined the *World League of American* Football and represented the Scottish Claymores as a kicker in their *World Bowl '96* championship win, as well as playing for the *Hong Kong Sevens*. In 2007, Hastings took up a post as chairman of Edinburgh Rugby, a club founded in 1872 and one of only two Scottish professional Rugby Union teams. He was inducted into the *International Rugby Hall of Fame*, with a career that included some of Scottish Rugby's greatest moments and a reputation as a forceful fullback capable of storming across lines and kicking long distances. Gavin Hastings received an OBE for services to rugby in 2003.

THE INVINCIBLES

THIERRY LACROIX
FRANCE

When France's fly-half phenomenon, Thierry Lacroix, stepped out for the 1995 Rugby World Cup, he did so for the second time in the tournament's history, and his performance was outstanding from the first whistle. Only two years after making his international test debut as a fly-half, he played in the 1991 tournament, scoring two penalties in the quarter-finals against England and two penalties against Canada in the preliminaries. By 1995, he was a seasoned international player, and his tally reached four tries, six conversions and ten penalties in the pool-stage matches, and a further conversion and a whopping 16 penalties in the quarter, semi and third-place finals.

Thierry Lacroix and his twin brother Pascal played rugby together from the age of seven, and their careers developed in tandem, playing for their school, university and the Army, being separated only when Pascal suffered a knee injury and Thierry was called up for the French team as a reserve in 1988. Lacroix's domestic career began in earnest with French team *Union Sportive Dacquoise*, known colloquially as *US Dax,* but his unmistakable talent soon saw him making his international Test debut in Strasbourg against Australia in 1989. With one Rugby World Cup tournament under his belt, Lacroix scored a sensational 20 points in France's opening Five Nations Championship game in 1994. Very much a team player, Lacroix was successful in a goal-kicker/centre role, especially when switching from aggressive defender to focussed goal-kicker within a matter of moments.

In 1995, Lacroix started out on fire, scoring two tries, three conversions and three penalties against Tonga, who lost 38-10. Four days later, France met Ivory Coast, toppling them 54-18. In that match, Lacroix added another two tries, two conversion and two penalties to his tally, before the third of France's pool-stage matches against Scotland. With a much tougher contest on their hands, France son 22-19, and Lacroix managed a conversion and five penalties – one of only two scorers in the match. In the quarter-finals, Ireland was no match for the French, losing 36-12 in a contest that had Lacroix taking a conversion and eight penalties. Meeting and losing to South Africa in the semi-finals, Lacroix was France's only point-scorer, with five penalties. In the play-off for third place, France beat England 19-9, and Lacroix took three penalties.

Following the 1995 Rugby World Cup, Thierry Lacroix was recruited into South Africa's *Natal Sharks*, playing in two *Currie Cups* before heading off to England. Retiring from international rugby in 1997, he joined *Harlequin FC* and then *Saracens FC*, leaving the latter in 2000 to head home and play for French team *USA Perpignan*. Juggling dual careers of rugby professional and physiotherapist, Lacroix finally retired from *Castres Olympique* club in 2000 at the age of 37. Upon his retirement, Thierry Lacroix had 43 caps and 367 points for France, with a record 112 points amassed in the 1995 Rugby World Cup alone.

THE INVINCIBLES

GONZALO QUESADA

ARGENTINA

When Gonzalo Quesada and his team readied themselves for the 1999 Rugby World with captain Lisandro Arbizu at the helm, *Los Pumas* knew that they were ready to take on the world's best – it was the rest of the rugby world who were in for a shock. Quesada, Argentina's fly-half, had made his Test debut three years earlier against the United States. 1999 was his first Rugby World Cup Tournament, and what a tournament it was! Argentina made the quarter-finals in an upset win over Ireland, and 25-year-old Quesada made history as the highest point scorer of the entire tournament.

Quesada's rugby career began in Buenos Aires, where he played for the *Hindú Club*, winner of the nation's *National de Clubes* domestic tournament in 1996 and home of Nicolas and Juan Fernández. In that year, Quesada was recruited into Argentina's national squad, and at 22-years-old, he debuted for Argentina against the United States. Quesada was part of a squad that had moved from amateurish roots in 1987 to a team worthy of inclusion at the competition's highest level. During the tournament, Gonzalo Quesadas' unusual goal-kicking technique was targeted by the English press, who dubbed him *Speedy Gonzalo* because of the lengthy time it took him to kick the ball. The English press stopped laughing when he scored 102 points in five games!

Up against Wales, Samoa and Japan in the pool-stage of the tournament, Quesada struck out early, scoring six penalties against Wales in Argentina's first match. Although the team went down to the Welsh, the margin was only 23-18, and Quesada was the only scorer for his side. The next match saw Argentina take Samoa 32-16, with Quesada again dominating with eight penalties and a drop-goal. In the final pool-stage game of the tournament, it was Japan who fell 33-12 to Argentina, and Quesada who took seven penalties. Pipped by Samoa for second place in the pool, Argentina faced Ireland in the newly created quarter-final play-offs, vying for a berth in the quarter-finals. With Quesada taking a conversion and seven penalties, and fellow countryman Diego Albanese scoring a try, Ireland managed seven penalties and a drop goal, losing 28-24 to Los Pumas.

At this point in the tournament, everybody's gaze was aimed at Argentina and its fly-half, and when the opening whistle sounded in Dublin for a quarter-final match against France, the outcome was anybody's guess. Argentina fell 47-26 to France, but not before Quesada took two conversions and three penalties, and Argentina stamped its authority on the game and left the rugby world in no doubt that their rugby star was rising.

After 1999, Quesada was recruited to French team *Racing Club de Narbonne* Méditerannée , and he remained in France, joining Béziers, Stade Français, Pau and Toulon. He also played for Argentina in the 2003 Rugby World Cup tournament, taking nine conversions, four penalties and a drop-kick. In 2007, Quesada returned to his home club, Hindú in Argentina, before taking up a directorship for Stade Français. In December, 2014, the Argentinian fly-half with 38 international caps and 486 points to his name renewed his contract as Sporting Director with Stade Français.

THE INVINCIBLES

JONAH LOMU

NEW ZEALAND

When the All Blacks lined up for their first match of the 1999 Rugby World Cup, Jonah Lomu was already well on his way to becoming Rugby Union's first global superstar. Having taken seven tries in the five matches that he played in the 1995 tournament, there was little doubt that Lomu, with youth and far more experience on his side, would prove to be a more formidable enemy that he had been four years previously. What nobody knew at the time was that Jonah Lomu suffered from a chronic kidney disease, and between cup matches in 1995, he had spent most of his time in bed recovering from his superhuman feats.

Lomu's domestic career for New Zealand began in 1993, when he played as an under-19. The following year, he played as an under-21, as well as in the *Hong Kong Sevens,* when the entire rugby world sat up and took notice of the teenager's incredible, natural talent. Less than two months after his 19th birthday, Lomu made his All Blacks debut against France in the first of two losing matches in New Zealand. A year later, he was in the 1995 Rugby World Cup squad, where he dazzled the rugby world with a scintillating performance that led many rival captains to label him a rugby *freak*. At 6' 5" and 120kgs, at his peak, Lomu took only 11 seconds to run 100 metres – something unheard of in such an enormously built athlete.

Lomu's first game for the 1999 tournament was against Tonga, and he scored the first two tries of his tournament total of eight. Six days later, he took another try against England in a match won by the All Blacks, and yet another two in the last of the pool-stage matches against Italy, who lost 101-3. In the quarter and semi-finals, he added three more tries to his tally before New Zealand lost to France and then to South Africa in the play-off for bronze. On the back of his earlier 1995 tournament performance, Jonah Lomu was without doubt the sensation of World Cup rugby, but it might never have happened given his medical condition. In 1996, his health issues reached a point that saw him miss most of the 1997 season, and it was only his ability to recover that saw him match fit for 1999.

After the 1999 tournament, Jonah Lomu struggled with his health between bouts of sensational rugby. In 2002 he was forced to step down from the All Blacks, and by 2003, he was on dialysis, receiving a donor kidney a year later. Within 12 months, Lomu began the climb back to international rugby, but a shoulder injury hampered his efforts at first. Eventually, he signed with Welsh team Cardiff, but a season-ending broken ankle cut short his intent, and within two years he was back playing in New Zealand. In 2007, Jonah Lomu retired from rugby, but he took part in charity matches and ultimately signed with the *Marseille Vitrolles* in France until 2010.

Lomu was diagnosed with nephrotic syndrome, a serious kidney disorder in 1995, and the disease had a significant impact on his playing career and wider life. By 2003 he was on dialysis and in 2004 underwent a kidney transplant. He then attempted a comeback but did not play international rugby again, and retired from professional rugby in 2007. He died unexpectedly on 18 November 2015 after suffering a heart attack associated with his kidney condition.

THE INVINCIBLES

MATT BURKE

AUSTRALIA

Matt Burke's path to the 1999 Rugby World Cup was strewn with injury and controversy, and he had only recently recovered from major surgery to remedy a shoulder injury a year earlier. Burke's inclusion in the side was almost as surprising as his form in the tournament itself, as he had been the subject of tension and speculation for some time, but a media campaign entitled *Bring Back Bill* saw him included in the squad. Had there been any doubt as to the Australian's ability to sizzle before the tournament, there was none when the Wallabies took the Webb Ellis Cup, with Burke a major, contributing factor in that victory.

Long thought to be the best international fullback in the game's history, Burke first came to prominence when selected to tour the United States and Ireland with the Australian Schoolboys team in 1990. He also began playing for his local club, Eastwood, in the same year, and he remained with them until 1996. Burke then played for Australia's Under 21s in 1992-3, while concurrently representing the *Hong Kong Sevens* in 1992 and the *Rugby World Cup Sevens* in the following year. At the same time, Burke was selected for his debut in a Test side, which was played against the Springboks. As a starting full-back and kicker, Burke set the game of rugby alight with his skill, and he was instrumental in many *Bledisloe Cup* wins in the ensuing years.

Having reached the 1995 tournament, there was still a reasonable amount of doubt about Burke's ability to perform to his best, but as the whistle sounded for the first of Australia's pool-stage matches, Burke set the rugby world on fire. The Wallabies' first match was against a much lower ranked Romania, who lost 57-9 in a match that saw Burke score a try and five conversions. Next, Australia faced and beat Ireland convincingly, and Burke added another two conversions and two penalties to his name. In the last of the tournament's pool-stage matches, Burke took a try, five conversions and a penalty, silencing the last of his critics. In the quarter and semi-finals, the points kept coming for Matthew Burke, with 11 conversions and a penalty, but he saved his best for last in the final against France – with two tries and seven penalties, Burke became Australia's deadliest weapon against France, taking two conversion and seven penalties in a 35-12 victory that gave the Wallabies the Web Ellis Cup.

After the 1999 Rugby World Cup, Burke's form began to suffer as a result of recurring injuries and lengthening recovery times, and he retired from Test rugby and headed for England. There, he played for the *Newcastle Falcons*, captaining the side and receiving a *Player of the Year* award. In 2008, Burke retired, but his legacy of 81 caps and 878 points for Australia, as well as his ability to carve up the opposition in blistering form will live on in the memory of Australia's best rugby moments.

THE INVINCIBLES

DOUG HOWLETT

NEW ZEALAND

Doug Howlett's place in New Zealand's 2003 Rugby World Cup was never in doubt. As one of the nation's top wingers, and with an already impressive international scoring record over the previous three years, Howlett had already shared the wing with Jonah Lomu. In the absence of Lomu in 2003, Howlett was thus perfect for the task at hand. Howlett took six tries in the pool-stage of the 2003 tournament, with a turn of speed that often left the opposition clutching at thin air.

Doug Howlett's rugby career began when he attended Auckland Grammar, where he successfully juggled rugby, athletics and school leadership positions. Making his first-class debut for Auckland at the age of 18, he found himself making his *Super 12* debut the following year for the *Highlanders* and finished the 1990s as a top New Zealand Colts player. In 2000, Howlett debuted internationally for the All Blacks, scoring a try with his first touch in a match against Tonga. He didn't pull on the black jersey again until the end of the season, when he went on tour and scored tries in each of New Zealand's three international matches. From there, Howlett shared the wing with a number of notable All Black players, including Jonah Lomu and Jeff Wilson – both record holders, but as he came into his own, he was used more frequently as a key player.

In his first Rugby World Cup, Howlett entered the fray as a player of note immediately – scoring two tries in a 70-7 drubbing of Italy. In the third and fourth of New Zealand's pool-stage matches, Howlett scored another two tries in each of the games against Tonga and Wales. The All Blacks ultimately fought it out with France in the battle for third place, and Howlett was one of the six try scorers in their 40-13 victory in Sydney, Australia.

Since 2003, Howlett has been an absolute champion for New Zealand, but in a team filled with other champions, he found himself being rested in favour of others. In 2006, he played an entire season with Auckland, but he was again selected for the Rugby World Cup squad. In that tournament, his form was at its peak, but he was rested for the quarter-final game against France as part of a scheme to introduce him into the semi-finals fresh. Sadly, the All Blacks didn't make the semi-finals, and Howlett's disappointment was understandable.

Following the frustration of the 2007 Rugby World Cup, Howlett launched the *Doug Howlett Outreach Foundation,* an organisation dedicated to assisting talented 8-14-year-olds with school and sports fees and expenses. He left the All Blacks and signed for the Irish team, *Munster*, where he remained for five years, taking 114 caps and 175 points and playing in the *Super 14* and *Heineken Cup* tournaments. Taking the captaincy in 2012, Howlett remained with Munster until his retirement in 2013, brought about by a shoulder injury. Howlett currently acts as a Corporate Ambassador in the Munster province.

THE INVINCIBLES

FRÉDÉRIC MICHALAK

FRANCE

Two years before the 2003 Rugby World Cup, Frédéric Michalak made his international debut for France against South Africa as a 19-year-old fly-half, and in those two short years he racked up a host of international matches. Although France fell in the semi-finals to England, Michalak was outstanding in his tournament debut, having scored his first international try earlier in the year in the *Six Nations* tournament against Italy in Rome.

Frédéric Michalak's rugby career began in his home town of Toulouse, France, debuting for *Stade Toulousain* at 16-years old in 1998. Three years later, Toulouse won the French Championship and Michalak was recruited to represent France internationally against South Africa. France won the match comfortably, and Michalak's performance was such that he lined up a week later to play Australia in the scrum-half position. Landing a penalty goal in a match that France won by a single point clinched Michalak's future as an international player, and he spent the ensuing two years playing in most of France's *Six Nations* tournaments. In 2003, before he took his place in the Rugby World Cup squad, Michalak played two *Six Nations* matches, and was instrumental in Toulouse's victory in the 2002-03 *Heineken Cup*. He played more test matches in the months before the whistle sounded to signify the start of the 2003 Rugby World Cup, and from that point on, he starred for his country with a talent that saw him score 101 points – second under Jonny Wilkinson's 113 points.

In the first of France's pool-stage matches, they faced Fiji, and Michalak scored an outstanding 26 points, taking four conversions and six penalties. In the ensuing match against Japan, Michalak scored a try, five conversions and three penalties, as well as a try, three conversions, four penalties and a drop against Scotland. France rested Michalak for the fourth of their pool-stage matches against the much lower-ranked United States, and he emerged fresh for the quarter-finals against Ireland. In that match, Michalak's stunning form continued, and he took four conversions and a penalty in a convincing win. It was in the semi-finals that France fell, with Michalak scoring only a single conversion in a game that saw him frustrated by an inaccurate boot and dominated by England's Jonny Wilkinson.

Michalak went from strength to strength after the 2003 tournament, starring in France's *Six Nations* fixtures and instrumental in Toulouse taking the 2004-05 *Heineken Cup*. Until 2007, Michalak was busy winning international and national, and he was included in the 2007 Rugby World Cup squad. In 2008, Michalak signed with the *Sharks*, a South African *Super Rugby* team, but injury forced him home to France after a win in the *Currie Cup*. Back in France, he signed with *RC Toulonnais*, but injury continued to plague Michalak, and within the year, he was back in South Africa again before being recalled to France for an international test against Argentina. With his objective to represent France internationally, Michalak again joined *RC Toulonnais* and played in their successful 2013 *Heineken Cup* win.

THE INVINCIBLES

MILS MULIAINA

NEW ZEALAND

All Blacks player Mils Muliaina had only made his international test debut four months before the 2003 Rugby World Cup, but he did so as a player destined to become one of New Zealand's most consistent and talented players in their international history. As a steady full-back, Muliaina could play wither wing or centre, and he had a rugby maturity about him that set him apart from others of his age. By the end of the 2003 tournament, Muliaina proved that a long history of playing at a high level throughout his teen years was the key to his success in 2003 and well beyond it.

Muliaina's rugby career began when he won a scholarship with an Auckland boy's secondary school, and he went on to play for the *New Zealand Secondary Schools XV*. With one world championship under his belt, Muliaina then advanced to repeat his success with the Under-19 and Under-21 teams, with three more championships won. With his future looking rosy, Muliaina was signed to the *Auckland Blues* in 2001, and two years later, he made his international test debut for New Zealand against England. Already a well-seasoned national *Sevens* player since 1999, Muliaina's entry into the 2003 Rugby World Cup was timely, because he was about to hit a peak that would last for some years to come.

If the All Blacks' opposition thought that New Zealand without Jonah Lomu would be an easier contest, they were mistaken. From the outset, New Zealand shone, and in their second match against Canada in the pool-stage of the tournament, Muliaina took four tries. A week later, he scored another two tries against Tonga, and as New Zealand battled it out for bronze against France, he scored yet another. Muliaina and Doug Howlett each topped New Zealand's try scoring table, with seven a piece for the tournament, and Muliaina's future as an All Black was set.

After his Rugby World Cup Debut, Muliaina went on to become the only New Zealand player selected for every one of the All Blacks' 2004 tests. A dominant member of the *Sevens* and *Super Rugby* teams, Muliaina played tests for New Zealand against 16 nations in his career, and scored tries against all but three of them. Ultimately, he captained his country against Italy and France in 2009 and played in a total of three Rugby World Cups. In 2011, Muliaina fractured his shoulder in his 100th game for New Zealand, and left the field at half time. The following day, he announced his retirement from the squad, but he was able to accept his gold medal when New Zealand won the 2011 Web Ellis Cup.

Since then, the fullback with 100 caps and 185 points to his name in a stellar international career, has played for Japan's *NTT DR Hurricanes* and was contracted with Ireland's *Connacht Rugby and The San Francisco Rush*.

THE INVINCIBLES

BRYAN HABANA

SOUTH AFRICA

The 2007 Rugby World Cup's top try scorer was Bryan Habana, with an impressive eight tries in his seven tournament appearances. Having made his international test debut for the Springboks three years earlier, Habana had already been named in the short-list for the 2005 *IRB World Player of the Year*, and was named 2005 *South Africa Player of the Year*. In the year leading up to the tournament, South Africa had suffered four losses in six of their *Tri Nations* matches, as well as test losses to Ireland, France and England. In the Ireland test, Habana was used at centre for the Springboks, and although he scored a try, South Africa lost. Habana's readiness for the 2007 tournament came not from his test losses, but from his success as Wing for South Africa's *Bulls* earlier in the year, and there was no doubt that it paid off for him.

Bryan Habana's rugby career began in 2003 when he played for the *Golden Lions* in the Currie Cup. A year later, he debuted in the South African Under-21 squad, as well as the *South African Sevens* for the 2003-04 *World Sevens Series*. Finally, at the age of 21 in late 2004, Habana debuted as a test international in a reserve capacity. By the end of that year, Habana had scored an impressive three tries from three test matches. Moving from the *Lions* to the *Blue Bulls* in 2005, Habana was also included in the Springbok's 2005 line-up, and he spent the next two years building his profile and equalling Doug Howlett and Joe Rokocoko's *Tri Nations* try-scoring points for the 2005 tournament. The Springbok's disappointing 2006 season gave rise to Habana's stellar performance in early 2007 during the *Super 14* season.

As wing in the Springbok's first 2007 Rugby World Cup game, Habana scored four tries against Samoa and a further two against the United States in the pool-stage round. In the semi-finals, he scored another two tries against Argentina, and played in South Africa's winning final against England under captain John Smit. Bryan Habana equalled Jonah Lomu's eight-try record as a result of tournament, cementing his place as a Springbok great.

In 2008, Habana suffered a slump in form, taking only two tries for the year, but the slump was South Africa's under a new coach, rather than one individual's poor form. In 2009, Habana's form returned during the British and Irish Lions' tour, and Habana celebrated his 50th test in the ensuing *Tri-Nations* tournament, which South Africa won. It was an especially fine victory for Habana, as it meant that he had won every tournament in the Southern Hemisphere in his career to date. In 2011, Habana joined the Springboks for the Rugby World Cup to take a try against Namibia and another against Samoa in the pool-stage matches. The Springboks made the quarter-finals but lost to Australia.

Habana continued to shine in international tests, and after a shift in domestic South African teams, he announced his move to French club *RC Toulonnais* in 2013.

THE INVINCIBLES

FELIPE CONTEPOMI
ARGENTINA

When Felipe Contepomi arrived at the 2007 Rugby World Cup, he was only a year away from inheriting Argentina's captaincy from Agustín Pichot – the nation's longstanding rugby champion. Contepomi and his twin brother, Manuel, were veterans of the 1999 and 2003 tournament squads when they readied themselves for what would be Argentina's most outstanding Rugby World Cup yet. As a new father and a newly graduated medical doctor, 2007 was about to become the stage upon which Felipe Contepomi starred, as the tournament's second-highest points scorer and a subsequent contender in the *2007 International Player of the Year* behind South Africa's Bryan Habana.

As fly-half, Contepomi's rugby career began in Buenos Aires, and by 1998, he was a member of Argentina's international squad. Having played Under-19s, Under-21s and Sevens at international level, he debuted against Chile in 1998 and went on to play internationally for his nation for the ensuing 15 years – taking 87 caps and 651 points. In the following year, he managed a conversion in a pool-stage match against Japan for the 1999 Rugby World Cup. Contepomi signed with English club *Bristol* in 2001, but transferred to *Leinster* in Ireland following Bristol's relegation in the 2002-03 season. With the 2003 Rugby World Cup looming, Contepomi scored 25 points in a winning international against Wales, before joining the RWC tournament for three of Argentina's four pool-stage games. In the years between 2003 and 2007, Contepomi featured heavily in international wins over England and France, as well as being instrumental in Leinster's *2005-06 Heineken Cup* win and becoming the top scorer in that tournament and the *2005-06 Celtic League*.

It was in 2007 that Contepomi came into his own and starred in Argentina's stunning performance at the 2007 Rugby World Cup. In a first match against France, Contepomi played inside-centre and took five penalties in an upset 17-12 win over France. In the ensuing 33-3 win over Georgia, he scored a conversion and three penalties, and then went on to take a try, four conversions and two penalties against Namibia in a 63-3 win. As Ireland fell to Argentina in a clean-sweep of the pool-stage, Contepomi added another conversion and three penalties to his tally before proceeding to the quarter-finals. In yet another upset, Argentina beat Scotland 19-13, with Contepomi taking a conversion and three penalties, and the Contepomi brothers were the only scorers in Argentina's semi-final loss to South Africa. Meeting France for a second time, Argentina won the bronze play-ff 34-10, and Contepomi dominated play, scoring a try, three conversions and a penalty. Although South African players took out the top scorer and most tries scored in the tournament, Contepomi took second in the most points scored.

With the international captaincy his, Contepomi featured heavily in Argentina's international ensuing victories, but in 2009, a knee injury sidelined him while playing for Leinster in a *Heineken Cup* semi-final. He returned in 2010, taking France internationally in a *Six Nations* championship and moving to French clubs *RC Toulonnais* and *Stade Français* before returning to Argentina in 2013. At that point, Contepomi announced his retirement from rugby, having played the most test matches in Argentina's history and having scored the most points in international games.

THE INVINCIBLES

JONNY WILKINSON

ENGLAND

Jonny Wilkinson was already a rugby-household name when the 2007 Rugby World Cup kicked off, having scored 71 points in the 1999 tournament and a massive 113 points in 2003. An ankle injury in the training run-up to the tournament rendered him benched for the first of the two pool-stage matches, but Wilkinson was no stranger to injury at that point in his career. From 2001 to 2006, he had suffered a total of 10 serious injuries to his legs, arms, shoulders and knees – as well as having endured surgery for a sportsman's hernia and appendicitis. He would go on to play a critical role in England's defence for the tournament, and by the time England was knocked out by South Africa in the final, he would become the tournament's highest point-scorer, with a total of 231 points!

Wilkinson's rugby career began as inside-centre for the *Newcastle School of Rugby* in England, and year later, he was recruited into the England squad at 18-years-old – England youngest ever international rugby player. His early international career included test, friendly and *5 Nations* matches, and by the time the 1999 Rugby World Cup dawned, he had already amassed 100 test points. Between 1999 and 2003, Wilkinson's international experience grew to include a stint as captain against Ireland for one of the *Six Nations Championship* matches. England won the Grand Slam, and in an ensuing Southern Hemisphere tour, Wilkinson scored all 15 points in a 15-13 win over New Zealand. With the next stop the 2003 Rugby World Cup, Wilkinson broke the record books and England won the Webb Ellis Cup. Replacing Lawrence Dallaglio as England's Captain the following year, Wilkinson's career ebbed and flowed with injuries, but when he was able to play, he was scintillating.

Missing the first two games of the 2007 tournament under captain Martin Corry, Wilkinson had to witness England's devastating 36-0 loss to South Africa from the bench. In the next game against Tonga, Wilkinson scored two conversions, two penalties and two drop-kicks, and England reached the quarter-finals. In a match that saw only Wilkinson scoring, England beat Australia 12-10. In the semi-finals, Wilkinson took another two penalties and drop kick to down France 14-9. Beaten 15-6 by South Africa in a try-less final, England's only scorer was Wilkinson, with two penalties.

In the following year, Wilkinson became the top points-scorer in the *Six Nations Championship* before surrendering to shoulder surgery. He returned to the *Guinness Premiership* for the *Newcastle Falcons* and after recovering from ankle and knee injuries, he signed with French team *RC Toulonnais*. Returning between injuries to play test rugby, Wilkinson became the second player in history, and the first in England, to achieve 1000 test points. After two years in France and with a litany of successful international wins behind him, Wilkinson retired from international rugby in 2011, but remained with *RC Toulonnais* until May, 2014. Jonny Wilkinson's rugby career was literally record breaking, and in 2011, he released his fifth book, entitled, *Jonny: My Autobiography*.

THE INVINCIBLES

PERCY MONTGOMERY

SOUTH AFRICA

South Africa's Percy Montgomery was without doubt the individual star of the 2007 Rugby World Cup, scoring 105 points and taking top honours in his own career and as a member of the tournament's winning squad. When he retired the following year, Montgomery did so as the Springbok's all-time caps and points record holder. As he took his place in the squad for the 2007 tournament, Montgomery celebrated a decade of international rugby for the Springboks, having played in the 1999 squad. He also managed another milestone during the tournament, when he reached a stellar 600 points in his international career, the first Springbok to do so, and then went on to surpass 700 points in the match against Mau Samoa.

Montgomery's international rugby career began in 1997, when he earned his first international cap as a 23-year-old outside-centre against the *British and Irish Lions*. Two years later, he featured in the 1999 Rugby World Cup for the Springboks, taking two drop-goals in the play-off win against New Zealand for third place. In 2002, having played domestically for *Western Province* and the *Stormers* in the *Currie Cup* and *Super Rugby* respectively, Montgomery moved to Wales to join *Newport RFC*, which would later become the *Newport Gwent Dragons*. At the time, the move to Wales ruled Montgomery out of contention for the 2003 Rugby World Cup, as he was only eligible for inclusion in the squad if he was playing domestically in South Africa. In 2003, Montgomery endured a two-year ban for assaulting a touch judge, with 18 months suspended and a return to Welsh rugby in December of that year. In 2004, Montgomery was recalled to the Springbok's squad after a rule change, and until 2007, he slowly rid himself of his early-career reputation for being erratic, playing for the *Natal Sharks* in the *Super 14* season.

South Africa began the 2007 tournament in blistering fashion, and Montgomery scored two tries, five conversions and three penalties in a 59-7 win over Samoa. The Springbok's next match saw England scoreless against South Africa, with Montgomery taking three conversions and four penalties. With another conversion and a penalty against Tonga, and six conversions and a penalty against the United States, Montgomery's points continued to grow in the quarter and semi-finals. Taking three conversions and a penalty against Fiji in the quarters, he amassed another four conversions in the semi-finals. Beating England to win the Webb Ellis Cup, it was Montgomery who starred in the final, with a massive four penalties.

After his performance in the 2007 tournament, Montgomery moved to France and joined *USA Perpignan* for a year, before returning to South Africa to play for the *Stormers* and *Western Province* in a reprisal of his 2002 role. Retiring as a player from the Springboks in 2008, Montgomery became a kicking consultant. In 2009, he concluded his plating career at the close of the 2009 *Super 14* season.

In all, Percy Montgomery won 102 caps and 893 points with the Springboks, took 79 caps and 430 points in super rugby, and 68 caps in domestic rugby, with a total 383 points scored. For the Welsh and French teams he joined, he won a combined total of 69 caps and 553 points.

THE INVINCIBLES

JAMES O'CONNOR

AUSTRALIA

James O'Connor burst onto the international rugby scene in 2008 as an 18-year-old full-back, and by the time the 2011 Rugby World Cup dawned, he was one of the most talked about Australian players. Having debuted brilliantly against Italy three years earlier, he was already being lauded as one of the Wallabies' most gifted youngsters. It was hard to believe that at the age of 16, he had fought for his life after boarding-school horseplay turned deadly and ruptured his spleen. Six weeks after his spleen was removed, the plucky teenager was back playing rugby, becoming *Super 14* rugby's youngest ever debutante before the year was out!

In 2011, O'Connor's international career was only three-years-old, but his involvement with rugby stretched back to his days as a youngster at *Nudgee College* in Brisbane, Australia. After the infamous spleen incident, O'Connor played in the national *Australian Schoolboys* team in 2007, and by 2008, he was playing for the national *Sevens* team. Debuting in *Super Rugby* at the age of 17 years for *Western Force*, O'Connor became a Wallaby at 18 – the second youngest player to ever don the green-and-gold jersey. 2008 was a big year for O'Connor, who played his first *Super 14* match in the season's 10th week and continued to finish the season as an inside-centre. Making his Wallabies debut later in the year, he played as a replacement fullback and scored three tries against Italy. In 2009, he won *Rookie of the Year* for both the Wallabies and *Western Force*.

As the 2011 Rugby World Cup began, experts the world already knew about O'Connor, but it was his performance over the ensuing weeks of the tournament that would propel him into the international spotlight. The versatile 21-year-old began his run by taking a try and three conversions in a win against Italy in the first of Australia's pool-stage matches. Next, O'Connor scored the only points in a losing match against Ireland, with two tries, before being rested for the match against the United States. In the last of the Wallabies' four preliminary matches, O'Connor took an incredible nine conversions against Russia, in a game that their opponents lost 68-22. The quarter-final bout against South Africa was a tough one, but O'Connor managed two penalties in a low-scoring 11-9 win over the Springboks. In the semi-finals, New Zealand relegated Australia to the play-off for third place, with O'Connor taking the Wallabies' only try. Up against Wales in a closely fought game, O'Connor scored a conversion and two penalties, and Australia won bronze.

In 2012, O'Connor made the move from *Western Force* to the Melbourne based *Melbourne Rebels*, but within the year, he found himself at the wrong end of some regretful but understandable incidents, and headed for England, joining *London Irish*. In 2014, he signed with French team, *RC Toulonnais,* and returned to Australia in 2015 to ready himself for inclusion in the 2015 Rugby World Cup squad. Upon his return, O'Connor also joined *Queensland Reds*, a *Super Rugby* team. O'Conner currently plays for Sale Sharks in the UK competition.

THE INVINCIBLES

VINCENT CLERC

FRANCE

With five tries for France in the 2007 Rugby World Cup, Vincent Clerc was favoured to excel in the 2011 tournament. Known for his history of multiple-try matches and an ability to snatch something from nothing on the wing, he was yet to hit the peak of his career, although his achievements over the past nine years in international rugby had been nothing short of spectacular. Among others, those achievements included five tries in two matches against Ireland and Scotland in the 2008 *Six Nations Championship*.

Clerc's rugby career began as a 17-year old with French team *FC Grenoble,* and by the time he was 21, he had moved to *Stade Toulousain* and also won his first cap for France as an international player. His first three international tries came almost immediately – one in a test match against South Africa, and two against Canada within the space of a fortnight. Having joined France's national team at a time when it was at its greatest strength, Clerc enjoyed success in the ensuing *Six Nations Championship* in 2003 and 2004, and further glory ensued in the lead-up to the 2007 Rugby World Cup. In the pool-stage round, Clerc scored a personal-best three tries against the luckless Namibia and a further two against Ireland to cement his reputation as a star of the game. Scoring and featuring strongly in the 2008 *Six Nations Championship*, Clerc continued to build a reputation for himself and France as his tally and experienced climbed. Going into the 2011 tournament, he already had *Heineken Cup* wins for *Stade Toulousain* to his name (2003, 05 and 10), and a *Top 14* trophy. With his involvement, France has also won the 2004, 06 and 07 *Six Nations Championship*, and Clerc wasn't yet done.

Clerc tied with English full-back and wing, Chris Ashton, for the most tries scored in the 2011 tournament, and he began his tally by taking a try against Japan in France's first pool-stage match. A massive three tries against Canada ensued, and a try against Tonga completed Clerc's run-up to the quarter-finals. France equalled England's tries in the quarter-final, with Clerc taking one of his squad's two to complete his tournament record haul of six tries. This made Clerc the second French player to top the Rugby World Cup try-scoring list, equalling Jean-Baptiste Lafond's 1991 shared tournament record.

Since 2011, Clerc has continued to represent *Stade Toulousain* as a winger, and he has amassed 298 caps and 620 points in his career with them. For France, he has 67 caps and 170 international points, scoring tries in eight separate test matches, eight *Six Nations Championship* appearances and six Rugby World Cup games. Clerc retired in 2018. Outside of the game, Vincent Clerc is associated with the French charity *Maison des Parents*, an organisation that works with the families of seriously ill children.

THE INVINCIBLES

MORNE STEYN
SOUTH AFRICA

When the Springboks' Morné Steyn took his place in the squad for the 2011 Rugby World Cup, he was already a rugby legend for South Africa. In his inaugural match against Wales, Steyn scored two conversions and a penalty, and so began a meteoric tournament for him – and a place in World Cup history as the top scorer of 2011. In the previous year alone, Steyn had taken and slotted every one of his 41 consecutive kicks during the *Castle Tri-Nations* tournament, as well as having taken the top points score for the Pretoria based *Bulls* in Super Rugby for the previous two seasons.

In 2011, Steyn was already a seasoned Currie Cup and Tri-Nations player, with a growing tally of national and international records under his belt. His professional rugby career began in 2003, when he joined the domestic club, *Blue Bulls* in Pretoria. It would take another six years before Steyn would make his Test debut against the British and Irish Lions in 2009. The greater talents of Ruan Pienaar and others had kept him from previous Test selection until then, but when Pienaar's form suffered a hiatus during the tour, Steyn stepped in as replacement and made a significant contribution from the beginning. The Springboks won that match, thanks to Steyn's last minute 53m penalty goal. Three months later, Steyn scored all 31 winning points against New Zealand in a *Tri-Nations* match.

South Africa expected great things from their favourite fly-half when the 2011 tournament began, and they weren't disappointed. Following the Springboks' win over Wales, Steyn took a try, five conversions and two penalties in a winning match against Fiji. The inexperienced Namibians fell 87-0 to South Africa next, and in that match, Steyn scored a try, six conversions and a penalty, playing alongside the man he had once replaced in his international Test debut – Ruan Pienaar. A conversion and a penalty against Samoa in the fourth of the Springbok's pool-stage matches saw the team and Steyn well placed to make history, but South Africa stumbled against Australia in the quarter-final and was bundled out of the tournament. Steyn however, managed two penalties and a drop goal, as well as becoming the tournament's top scorer (with 62 points) without the benefit of semi finals or finals exposure.

The name Morné Steyn is synonymous with breaking records in both domestic and international rugby. Some of his achievements include being the player to reach 100 points fastest as a Springbok, and to continue at century intervals up to 600 points – Steyn reached 600 points in only 50 Test matches. In Super Rugby, Steyn has consistently been the top drop-kick goal scorer, as well as the player scoring most penalties and overall points. In the history of Super Rugby in South Africa, Steyn maintains the record for the most points scored. In 2013, Morné Steyn joined France's illustrious *Stade Français*, and currently has 109 caps and 595 points to his name for them.

WORLD CUP TEAMS

ARGENTINA

Known as *Los Pumas*, Argentina has a rugby heritage that reaches back into the 19th century. In a country where football dominates as a national sport, rugby has been played since the 1870s, having arrived with migrants from Great Britain. South American rugby tournaments began in the 1950s, and Argentina dominated early on, eventually expanding their horizons and touring Rhodesia and South Africa in the mid 1960s. In the following decade, Argentina continued to tour, defeating Australia, England and France upon occasion.

Argentina has played in every Rugby World Cup, but it was in 1999 that they began to be considered as a serious contender for Web Ellis victory. Reaching the quarter-finals for the first time in that year, and the semi-finals in 2007, Argentina took bronze in the latter, stunning the international rugby world. Argentina currently sits 8th in the World Rugby Rankings.

Since the 2011 tournament, Argentina has joined the *Rugby Championship* (formerly the Tri Nations), pitting themselves against New Zealand, Australia and South Africa in a Tier 1 rugby competition.

1987
Argentina entered the competition as amateurs in 1987, losing 28-9 to Fiji in the first of their pool matches, before beating Italy 25-16. Their victory was short lived, as New Zealand dismissed them from the tournament with a 46-15 win.

1991
Argentina lost each of its pool matches against Australia, Wales and Western Samoa in 1991. They were unable to advance to the quarter-finals.

1995
Although Argentina failed to win a single match of its pool stage, their losing margin in al three games was a mere six points. Experts were now beginning to take the cup's only South American entrant more seriously, and the promise of what was to come in 1999 was on more than a few sporting minds.

1999
1999 saw Argentina the surprise heroes of the Rugby World Cup. An initial close-fought loss to Wales preceded a 32-16 win against Samoa and a 33-12 victory over Japan, sending Argentina to the newly introduced quarter-final play-offs. Ireland fell to Argentina in a match that surprised the rugby world, and catapaulted Argentina into the quarter-finals for the first time. A 47-26 loss against France ended their hopes for cup glory, but 1999 was nevertheless a victory over all for the plucky rugby nation.

2003
Argentina's potential as future rugby champions was evident in their 67-14 and 50-3 wins against Namibia and Romania respectively. A 24-8 loss to Australia was not unprecedented, but a tight, 16-15 loss to Ireland showed the world that Argentina has what it takes to reach the greater heights of world rugby. They did not advance to the quarter-finals in 2003.

2007
2007 showed the world that Argentina was now a serious, international rugby team. Winning all four pool stage matches, they faced and beat Scotland in the quarter-finals, but were knocked out by South Africa in the semi-finals. Argentina took on France in the battle for bronze, and won 34-10 in one of Rugby World Cup's greatest upsets.

2011
Argentina's winning margins continued to climb over the lower ranked nations in the pool stage matches, losing only to England in a tense, 13-9 match. In the quarter-finals, Argentina met New Zealand, but the All Blacks were too strong, winning 33-10 and bundling Argentina out of the competition.

2015

Argentina's second best result was fourth place in 2015 winning 4 matches beating Georgia 54-9, Tonga 45-16, Namibia 64-19, Ireland 43-20 in the Quarter Finals and eventually losing to Australia 15-29 in the Semi-Final.

AUSTRALIA

At number six in the World Rugby Rankings, Australia has a rugby pedigree that matches its English and Welsh counterparts. Known as the Wallabies, Australia first toured New Zealand in 1882, several years before a British rugby team arrived and Australia won the first test match 13-3. World War I put paid to rugby in Australia until the early 1930s, as did World War 2 until the late forties, when Australia again began touring internationally. Chequered fortunes followed the Wallabies throughout the sixties and seventies, but as the inaugural Rugby World Cup drew nearer, the rugby might of Australia gained momentum. In the history of the Web Ellis Cup, Australia has always advanced beyond the pool stage, and it has won the trophy twice.

1987
Australia beat England 19-6, Japan 60-7 and the United States 34-6 to advance unbeaten to the knockout quarter-finals of the inaugural Rugby World Cup. Facing Ireland for a place in the semi-finals, they downed their opponents 33-15 to advance. A 30-24 loss to France saw the Wallabies facing Wales in the battle for bronze, but the Welsh took the match by a single point.

1991
Early pool wins over Wales, Argentina and Western Samoa saw the Wallabies up against Ireland in the quarter-finals. Winning by a single point, Australia advanced to the semi-finals to beat New Zealand 16-6 and head for a final showdown with England in the final. A 12-6 victory saw the Wallabies victors and the cup yet to leave the Southern Hemisphere.

1995
On South African soil, the Wallabies fell to the Springboks in their inaugural 1995 Rugby World Cup appearance, but wins over Canada and Romania advanced Australia to the knock-out round. England Curtailed Australia's progress, defeating them 25-22 in one of many close run results of the tournament.

1999
The Wallabies were in fine form early, beating Romania 57-9, Ireland 23-3 and the United States 55-19. Leapfrogging over the new play-offs, Australia faced Wales in the quarter-finals, winning 24-9 to battle it out with the Springboks in the semi-final. A 27-21 win saw Australia reach the finals to face and defeat France 35-12 and take the Webb Ellis Cup.

2003
Australia beat Argentina 24-8, Romania 90-8 and Ireland 17-16 in three of its four pool stage matches. In a game against Namibia, the Wallabies set a still-existing record win in the 142-0 final score before advancing to the quarter finals. A 33-16 win over Scotland pushed Australia to a showdown with New Zealand in the semi-finals, and a 22-10 win that set them up against England in the final. England took the Web Ellis Cup 20-17.

2007
With four straight wins in the pool stage matches, Australia advanced to the quarter finals to face England. A 12-10 loss saw the Wallabies bundled out of a tournament that held many surprises.

2011
With strong wins against Russia, the United States and Italy, Australia lost 15-6 to Ireland, but amassed the points to advance to the quarter-finals. An 11-9 win over South Africa sent the Wallabies into the semi-finals, where they faced New Zealand and lost 20-6. A match against Wales for third place proved fruitful, with the Wallabies winning 21-18.

2015
Australia made it to the finals at the 2015 World Cup losing to New Zealand 34-17 at Twickenham Stadium, London. Winning all their group matches, Australia progressed to the Quarter Finals beating Scotland 35-34 in a thriller and easily beating Argentina 29-15 in the Semi Final.

CANADA

Unlike its North American neighbour, Canada has competed at every Rugby World Cup since 1987. The *Maple Leafs* took to rugby at the same time the United States did, and one of the first games played was an international between the USA's Harvard University and Canada's McGill University. Establishing their own Rugby Union, Canada adopted rules that differed from those in Europe, including the ability to pass forward – something that dominated American Football.

With rugby on hold during World Wars I and II, Canada eventually resumed its game, although it wasn't until the 1960s that they began touring seriously. While they were yet to reach the strength of their European and Southern Hemisphere counterparts, they nevertheless established themselves a rugby nation far superior to their northern neighbours.

Canada was invited to represent North America in the inaugural Rugby World Cup in 1987. Ten years later, they recorded their poorest RWC performance, but 2011 saw the *Maple Leafs* only just miss contention for automatic inclusion in 2015.

Canada's highest cap holder is Al Charron, a retired flanker with 76 caps. For his fourth Rugby World Cup tournament in 2003, Charron underwent a full knee reconstruction before taking his place as Canada's rugby captain. After defeating Tonga in that tournament, Charron retired as a player but attended the 2007 tournament as part of Canada's management team. Another Canadian rugby great is Winston Stanley, capped 66 times as a wing. Stanley debuted in the Rugby World Cup tournament in 1995, and retired after the 2003 tournament. Stanley now dedicates himself to coaching in Canadian schools.

1987
Wales and Ireland were too good for Canada in their pool matches, and a high-scoring win over Tonga left them with a solitary win in 1987, and elimination at the pool stage.

1991
An early 13-3 victory against Fiji and a subsequent 19-11 win over Romania saw Canada lose only one of its pool stage matches, but without 1987's high margins. Their inaugural quarter-final appearance saw Canada lose 29-13 to the All Blacks.

1995
Canada won only a single match in the pool stage round. Losing 27-11 to Australia and 34-3 to Romania, it was the 20-0 thrashing handed out by South Africa that saw an end to their hopes for 1995.

1999
Canada's two tries in the first of its pool stage matches were outclassed and doubled by France, who won 33-20. A loss to Fiji, followed by a very respectable 72-11 win over Namibia saw Canada depart the 1999 tournament.

2003
Losing 41-10 to Wales in their first pool stage match, Canada then fell 68-6 to New Zealand and, surprisingly, 19-14 to Italy. A resounding 24-7 defeat of Tonga lifted Canadian spirits regardless of their inability to make the quarter-finals.

2007
Canada's fortunes fell in 2007, losing three of its pool stage matches and drawing with Japan in the fourth. Canada were unable to advance to the quarter-finals.

2011
Beating Tonga 25-20 and drawing 23-23 with Japan was not enough to see Canada advance to quarter-finals contention in 20-11. A 79-15 loss to New Zealand and a 46-19 victory by France saw Canada unable to advance in the 2011 tournament.

2015
Canada put in a brave effort in 2015 but failed to get past the pool rounds losing to Ireland, Italy, France and Romania.

ENGLAND

The country from which the game of Rugby Union originated in the early 19th century currently sits fourth in the *World Rugby Rankings*. Their first international game was held 116 years before the inaugural Rugby World Cup, and in that time they have played in many championships against the world's leading rugby nations. Since 1910, Twickenham Stadium has been the home of Rugby League in England, and it is now the world's largest rugby-dedicated ground, with a capacity of over 82,000 spectators.

England has won the Rugby World Cup once, in 2003. Upon the team's return to England, an entire nation came out to celebrate, jamming London's thoroughfares to see their triumphant heroes transported in open topped buses to meet Queen Elizabeth at Buckingham Palace and the Prime Minister at Downing Street.

The nation's all-time champion point scorer was Jonny Wilkinson, with 91 caps and a stunning 1179 points. Wilkinson retired from the national team in late 2011, and from rugby altogether in 2014 – he is lauded as possible one of the world's best ever players of the sport.

1987
England went into the inaugural tournament to share a pool with Australia, who promptly won 19-6. Resounding wins over Japan and the USA saw England advance to the quarter-finals, where they met Wales and were beaten 16-3 and knocked out of the tournament.

1991
An early 18-12 loss to the All Blacks in the pools stage round was countered by a 36-6 victory over Italy and a 37-9 win against the United States. England advanced to the quarter-finals, beating France 19-10 and advancing to face Scotland in the semi-finals. A 9-6 victory over Scotland saw England and Australia battle it out in the Web Ellis Cup final, which was taken 12-6 by the Wallabies.

1995
England won all three of their pool stage matches, advancing to the quarter-finals to face Australia. A 25-22 victory over the Wallabies resulted in a showdown with New Zealand for finals contention, but the All Blacks took the match 45-19. Up against France for third place, England lost 19-9.

1999
A strong 67-7 victory over Italy preceded a 30-16 loss at New Zealand's hands in 1999, but England went on to beat Tonga 101-10 and advance to the quarter-final play-off stage (newly introduced in 1999). Beating Fiji 45-25, England then faced South Africa in the quarter-finals, losing 44-21 and departing the tournament.

2003
A resurgent England won all of its pool stage matches in 2003, advancing to the quarter-finals. Beating Wales 28-17, they advanced to the semi-finals to face France, who lost 24-7. England then faced Australia in the Web Ellis Cup final, winning 20-17 and taking the cup home to meet Queen Elizabeth.

2007
A surprise 36-0 loss to South Africa in the pool stage of the 2007 tournament sobered the reigning champions, but England advanced to the quarter-finals with three wins. A narrow 12-10 victory over Australia ensued, leaving England to face France in the semi-finals. Defeating France 14-9, it was an England-South Africa final, with the Springboks the clear victors with a 15-6 win.

2011
As in 2003, England won all of its pool stage matches to advance to the quarter-finals unbeaten. There, they faced France, only to lose 19-12 and retire from the 2011 tournament.

2015
England was the sole host of the 2015 Rugby World Cup, although eight games were held at the Millennium Stadium. England finished 3rd in Pool A despite beating Fiji and Uruguay leaving Australia and Wales to progress to the next round.

FIJI

Fiji has played in every Rugby World Cup but one since the tournament's inception. Known as the *Flying Fijians,* the country boasts Rugby Union as its national sport, and almost ten percent of the population is registered with a club. Fiji's limited size and geographical position had led to many of its top players taking international contracts in Europe, Australia and New Zealand, although earnings are repatriated to Fiji, and thus stimulate the economy.

The history of rugby in Fiji has its origins in the native constabulary in the late 19th century, when both Fijian and European soldiers played the game. As Fijian rugby advanced into the early 20th century, clubs were either exclusively European or Fijian, and it wasn't until 1924 that a true Fijian team was formed to play their first international game against Samoa. In the ensuing years, Fiji played Tonga, Samoa and eventually, New Zealand. At that point, Fijian players preferred to play without boots, such was their natural rugby ability. By 1939, Fiji had become the Pacific's strongest team, and a tour of New Zealand set a record that remains today.

The Oceania competition for a berth in the Rugby World Cup has always been fierce, but apart from 1995, Fiji has played in all of them. They have reached the quarter-finals twice and the quarter-final play-offs once, and apart from their 2011 performance against Wales, they have performed well in most of their pool stage matches. Fiji currently sits 12th in the World Rugby Rankings.

Hooker Sunia Koto is Fiji's most experienced player, with 38 caps for Fiji and two caps for the Pacific Islanders. Koto debuted for Fiji in 2005 and played in four 2007 Rugby World Cup games for his country.

1987

Fiji won only one of its pool matches in the inaugural cup, but with highest number of tries, they advanced to the quarter-finals to face France. Knocked out by France, the margin was nevertheless a respectable 31-16.

1991

Failing to win any matches in the pool stage, Fiji nevertheless fought hard against Romania, losing 17-15 in a closely contested battle.

1995

Fiji failed to qualify for the 1995 Rugby World Cup.

1999

Beating Namibia 67-18 and Canada 38-22, Fiji fell 28-19 to France in the last of the pool stage matches in 1999. This sent them to the newly introduced quarter-final play-offs to face England, who beat Fiji 45-24.

2003

An early 61-18 loss to France preceded a single point win over the United States, before Fiji took Japan 41-13 and lost by two points to Scotland. They were unable to proceed to the quarter-finals.

2007

In 2007, Fiji won three of their four pool stage matches, beating Wales, Canada and Japan to advance to the quarter-finals. A 37-20 los to South Africa saw Fiji bundled out of tournament contention.

2011

An early 49-25 victory over Namibia was Fiji's high point in 2011. A 49-3 loss to South Africa, followed by a 27-7 downing by Fiji was capped off by a 66-0 result against Wales and the end of Fiji's involvement.

2015

Fiji finished behind England in their pool and failed to advance to the quarter finals at the 2015 World Cup.

FRANCE

Rugby reached France in the later 19th century from England, and the nation took to the new game with verve. In 1947, France played in the *Five Nations* tournament after a pre- World War II invitation was extended, and by the mid 1950s they shared dominance of the game with England and Wales. The quality and strength of French Rugby Union has grown continually since then, and they entered the inaugural Rugby World Cup as strong favourites. France has taken second in three Web Ellis Cup finals and has played for third place three times, winning bronze once.

1987
One of the biggest surprises of the inaugural cup was when France drew 20-20 in the first game of their pool. France went on to down Romania 55-12 and Zimbabwe 60-21 before advancing to the quarter-finals to face Fiji. A 31-16 win advanced them to the semi-finals, where they beat the Wallabies by six points to face New Zealand in the final. The All Blacks took the cup on home ground in a convincing 29-9 win over France

1991
France's pool matches against Fiji and Romania were easily won, but Canada put up a fight before losing 19-13. In the quarter-finals, France faced England, but they failed to advance after a 19-10 loss.

1995
Unbeaten in the pool stage, France walked over Tonga and Ivory Coast, while scoring a three-point victory over Scotland to advance into the quarter-finals. A solid 36-12 win over Ireland saw France face South Africa in the semi-finals. Losing 19-15 to the Springboks, France played England for bronze, winning 19-9 to take a respectable third in World Cup Rugby.

1999
Les Bleus took Canada 33-20, Namibia 47-13 and Fiji 28-19 to advance directly to the quarter-finals and avoid the new play-offs. A 47-26 win over heroic Argentina was the precursor to a 43-31 win against New Zealand in the semi-finals and a berth in the final against Australia. The Wallabies were too good for France, winning 35-12.

2003
Winning all of their pool stage matches, France advanced to the knockout quarter-final round to face Ireland, winning 43-21. A showdown with England in the semi-finals saw France lose 24-7 and vie against New Zealand for third place. The All Blacks took bronze in a 40-13 win over France.

2007
As hosts for 2007, France was the first team to discover Argentina's rising rugby talent. Losing 17-12, Les Bleus won the remaining three matches of their pool stage and advanced to the quarter-finals. Downing New Zealand 20-18, they faced England in the semi-finals and lost 14-9. A fight for bronze saw France and Argentina fight it out, with Argentina winning 34-10.

2011
France only two of its pool stage matches, but a draw with Japan saw them advance to the quarter-finals over Tonga. A 19-12 victory over England saw France advance to the semi-finals, where they beat Wales 9-8 and qualified for the final against New Zealand. Low scoring dominated the Web Ellis Cup final, and New Zealand won by a solitary point.

2015
France had a stunning World Cup with wins against Italy 32-10, Romania 38-11 and Canada 41-18 to advance to the Wuarter Finals. However, New Zealand put on a masterclass defeating France 62-13 at Millennium Stadium, Cardiff.

GEORGIA

Georgia's rugby heritage has grown out of a melee of failed attempts and political interference through the first half of the 20th century and into the 1980s. Most importantly, the game bears a strong resemblance to one of Georgia's ancient games – *Lelo Burti*. Centuries of placing a ball in the middle of a field, and then challenging two teams of village men to win the ball and carry it across a nearby creek, meant that Georgia was already a rugby team in waiting.

Organised Rugby Union began in Georgia in 1964, but as the country was part of the Soviet Union, it was Russia's own Rugby Federation that controlled the game. Ties to the French Communist Party meant that Georgia was able to play France, but continual poaching by Russia often left Georgia without its best players. Once Georgia seceded from the Soviet Union, they were determined to be a rugby nation in their own right, and they were finally admitted to the IRB in 1992. A hard fought qualification round in 1998 meant that Georgia missed out on playing in the 1999 Rugby World Cup, but a spectacular win in the *European Nations Cup* saw them qualify for the 2003 tournament. The final game that would decide the qualifier for 2003 was against Russia, and after national celebrations following a closely contested win, the Georgia national team was subjected to a controversial reshuffle.

Australian Milton Haig currently coaches Georgia's national squad. Past notable players include Ilia Zedginidze, who captained Georgia for the 2007 tournament. Zedginidze was forced to withdraw following an injury, and after a period of retirement, he returned to play in the 2009 *European Nations Cup*, scoring a try against Portugal to snatch victory. One of Georgia's best top scorers is Malkhaz Urjukashvili, who holds 65 caps, and a stunning tally of 42 conversions, 18 tries, 1 drop goal, 41 penalties and a 300 point aggregate. Georgia's bad-boy of rugby is Mamuka Gorgodze, a player renowned for his ability to collect yellow cards. Banned for fighting as a member of the French team, *Montpellier*, Gorgodze was nevertheless named man of the match twice during the 2011 Rugby World Cup – in games against Romania and Wales.

Although they have not yet made the Webb Ellis Cup quarter-finals, all indicators are that it is only a matter of time before they do.

2003
Losing 84-6 to England in the first of their pool stage matches, Georgia was trounced by Samoa, but held up well against South Africa before losing 46-19. A final 24-12 loss at the hands of Uruguay finished their 2003 cup hopes.

2007
Georgia fared well by downing Namibia 30-0, and managed a very respectable 14-10 loss to Ireland. Argentina and France however, were far superior, with Georgia losing 33-3 and 64-7 respectively and failing to advance to quarter-finals contention.

2011
A solitary win marked Georgia's 2011 tournament, scored against Romania. Losses of 15-6 to Scotland, 41-10 to England and 25-7 to Argentina ended Georgia's hopes for 2011 quarter-finals contention.

2015
Despite winning two of their pool games against Tonga and Namibia, Georgia failed to progress to the next rounds at the 2015 World Cup.

IRELAND

Ireland's rugby heritage is as ancient as its traditional game of *Caid* - an early football game that has been around since at least the 14th century, and from which rugby and Gaelic football arose. At number three in the World Rugby Rankings, and with five players earning *World Rugby Hall of Fame* induction, Ireland's national team is comprised of players from both the Republic of Ireland and Northern Ireland. Ireland's early Rugby League history was one chequered with notorious lows and sensational highs, but since trailing their Northern Hemisphere rivals through the 1960s, they have continued to improve and become a Rugby League force to be reckoned with. Since the advent of the Rugby World Cup in 1987, Ireland has continued to edge closer to the ultimate victory – one that might be only a heartbeat away in 2015.

Ireland's current coach is New Zealand's Joe Schmidt. Ireland's most capped player in history is Brian O'Driscoll, with 133 caps. In his career, O'Driscoll played 133 test matches for Ireland, captaining 83 and scoring 46 tries. He also played 8 test matches for the *British and Irish Lions*, and is Ireland's highest try scorer in history, the world's eighth-highest try scorer, and the highest-scoring centre in the history of international rugby.

1987
After an initial 13-6 loss to Wales, Ireland downed Canada 46-19 and Tonga 32-9 to advance into the quarter-finals. A tough game against Australia on Wallabies home soil saw Ireland bundled out of the tournament 33-15 in the knockout round.

1991
The first Rugby World Cup to be held in the Northern Hemisphere saw Ireland thunder through their first two matches, with a 55-11 win over Zimbabwe and a 32-16 victory over Japan. Scotland then scored a 24-15 win over Ireland, but they nevertheless advanced to the knockout round before going down to Australia in a nail-biting 19-18 result.

1995
Ireland faced the might of the All Blacks first up in the 1995 tournament, losing 43-19. A 50-28 victory over Japan lifted the spirits, but it was their last pool match that nobody in any doubt of Ireland's growing rugby might – they beat Wales 24-23. Advancing to the quarter-finals for the third time in three tournaments, Ireland eventually fell 36-12 to France and their Rugby World Cup was over for 1995.

1999
Ireland's ups and downs saw a spectacular 53-8 drubbing of the USA, but their subsequent 23-3 loss to Australia had a sobering effect. A convincing 44-14 win over Romania saw them advance to the newly introduced quarter-final play-offs, where Argentina took everybody by surprise and knocked Ireland out in a closely fought 28-24 win.

2003
Ireland again found itself in a pool against Australia in 2003, but after resounding wins against Romania and Namibia, and a one-point victory over Argentina, they faced the Wallabies as a side reborn. Australia won by a single point, and Ireland advanced into the quarter-finals to face France. A 43-21 loss might have bundled Ireland out of cup contention, but there was no doubt that the Shamrock was on the rise.

2007
2007 was Ireland's poorest performing Rugby World cup year, and only two wins in the pool matches saw them unable to advance to the quarter-final knockout round.

2011
A resurgent Ireland dominated its 2011 pool, advancing unbeaten to the quarter-finals and leaving the Wallabies with the memory of an unexpected 15-6 loss to Ireland. Knocked out by Wales 22-10, Ireland again failed to advance beyond the quarter-finals.

2015
Ireland topped Pool D of the 2015 Rugby World Cup with four victories and with two bonus points. Ireland beat Canada and Romania with bonus points in their first two games. Ireland then faced Italy, coming out on top 16–9,[5] the only try coming from Keith Earls who surpassed Brian O'Driscoll as Ireland's leading Rugby World Cup try scorer with eight. The final pool game saw Ireland face France. The winner would set up a quarter final against Argentina and avoid the All Blacks. Ireland overcame the loss to injury of key players Jonathan Sexton, Peter O'Mahony and Paul O'Connell to run out 24–9 winners.[6][7] The victory set up another game for Ireland in the Millennium Stadium against Pool C runners up Argentina on 18 October 2015. Ireland battled and came back from a 17-point deficit to come within 3 points of their opponents, but eventually lost 43–20.

ITALY

Since 1929, Italy have been passionate about rugby, and since 2000, they have competed in the *Six Nations Championship* against Wales, Ireland, France, Scotland and England. They play France annually for the *Guiseppe Garibaldi Trophy*, and they currently sit 15th in the World Rugby Rankings. Known as the *Azzuri* (Sky Blues), Italy has qualified for every Rugby World Cup since 1987, with improved performances indicating they have yet to reach their peak in the international arena.

It was the Allied troops in the immediate post WW2 war period who encouraged rugby to recommence in Italy, and since then, Italy has grown as a rugby nation. Recruiting international players and coaches in the 1970s and 1980s, Italy's national championship game improved, which in turn led to a better equipped national team in the *Six Nations Championship*. In 1987, Italy went into the Rugby World Cup as underdogs, but they nevertheless beat Fiji in the inaugural year, and their two pool stage victories in 2011 indicate that they are a rugby nation on the rise.

Italy is currently coached by Conor O'Shea. He played as a full back and occasionally at out-half and centre for Ireland, Lansdowne and London Irish. He has also coached London Irish and Harlequins, and held management positions with the English Rugby Football Union and the English Institute of Sport. Marcello Cuttitta holds the record for the most tries scored for Italy, with 25 tries and 54 caps. Cuttitta retired in 2000 after representing his nation in the 1987, 1991 and 1995 Rugby World Cups, and a career that included playing for L'aquila, Amatori Milan and Calvisano. The most points scored for Italy was by Diego Domínguez, who initially played Argentina before playing for Italy (through his grandmother's nationality). Along with only four other players in the history of international rugby, Domínguez has scored in excess of 1,000 points. He retired in 2000, but returned shortly afterwards, playing his final game in 2003.

1987
Italy, along with two other members of its 1987 tournament pool, won only a single match. With one less try than Fiji, they were unable to advance to the quarter-finals.

1991
Surprising the United States in a resounding 30-9 win, Italy lost 31-21 to New Zealand and 36-6 to England, seeing them knocked out of the tournament in the pool stage.

1995
An early 42-18 loss to Western Samoa was balanced by a respectable 27-20 loss against England and a 31-25 victory over Argentina in the pool stage matches on the 1995 tournament. Italy did not advance to the quarter-finals.

1999
Two terrifyingly large losses against England and New Zealand put paid to Italy's hopes for moving into the quarter-final play-offs, but their 28-25 loss to Tonga restored some pride before Italy were dismissed from the tournament.

2003
A 70-7 loss to New Zealand heralded the start to Italy's pool stage matches, but they recovered well enough to take Tonga 36-12 and Canada 19-14. A 27-15 loss to Wales saw Italy bundled out of quarter-finals contention.

2007
Apart from an expected rollercoaster loss to New Zealand, Italy fared well in 2007, with two wins in the pool stage matches. A closely contested 18-16 loss at Scotland's hands finished Italy's hopes for reaching the quarter-finals.

2011
Italy's fortunes rose in 2011, with a 53-17 victory over Russia and a 27-10 win over the United States. Losses of 32-6 against the Wallabies and 36-6 to Ireland saw Italy unable to advance to the quarter-finals.

2015
Italy secured a tough group in Pool D at the 2015 event with France and Ireland always destined to keep them out of the next rounds. Despite defeating Canada and Romania, Italy failed to progress to the Quarter Finals.

IVORY COAST

Ivory Coast, or *Les Éléphants* as they are known colloquially, first began playing rugby at a professional level in 1990, but the game itself has a history that began just after World War II. It was the French who introduced the game to the nation as a result of Côte d'Ivoire's time as a French Colony, but it was only when the Abidjan University adopted the game in the 1980s that it became popular. In 1986, the *Confederation of African Rugby* (CAR) was formed, and although Ivory Coast were not yet established as a national team, delegates attended the official launch. Determined to show the world that African rugby was more than just South Africa and its close Namibian and Zimbabwean allies, other CAR nations included Tunisia, Madagascar, Kenya, Tanzania and many others.

Although not a recognised rugby team when the inaugural Rugby World Cup was held, plans were already afoot for Ivory Coast to join the rugby elite in tournaments beyond the 1991 cup. The charge was led by François Dali, whose son, Athanese Dali, debuted for Ivory Coast in 1993 as fly-half, and Ivory Coast set its cap for the 1995 tournament in South Africa. Only one nation from the *Africa 1* pool was to achieve a place in the tournament, because South Africa was automatically included as the host nation. Ivory Coast played in Group B, Round 1 with Morocco and Tunisia, winning both of their games. In Round 2, they beat Namibia 13-12 and Zimbabwe 17-10, losing 17-9 to Morocco but finishing the leader of their qualifying group. To the surprise of many, Ivory Coast qualified for the 1995 tournament.

For the 1999 tournament, one direct and one *repechage* qualification were available, but in Round 4, Ivory Coast failed to win a single game and were eliminated. History repeated itself in the qualifying round for the 2003 tournament, and Ivory Coast fell to Tunisia and Morocco to bow out of contention. Ivory Coast won both of its Pool A games in Round 1b of the 2007 qualifying process, but subsequent losses to Uganda and Morocco ended their run for the cup. For 2011, initial wins against Morocco and Zambia sent Ivory Coast to the next round, but a draw with Namibia was not enough to gain the valuable aggregate points required to advance. For 2015, a single, aggregate point difference saw Ivory Coast fail in its bid to compete.

Players who have starred for Ivory Coast include Aboubakar Camara, a fly-half with 7 caps between 1993 and 1995. Camara played in the 1995 Rugby World Cup, scoring a try against France. Ismaila Lassissi, a loose-forward, also played for Ivory Coast between 1993 and 1995, with 8 caps. Current players include Jean-Maurice Oulouma, who spent his adult life playing rugby in France, but represents Ivory Coast as a wing or a centre. Fullback Silvère Tian also plays for a French team and has represented Ivory Coast internationally since 1997.

1995
An 89-0 loss to Scotland heralded Ivory Coast's entry into the tournament, although the 54-18 loss to France proved that the team was not a walkover. Ivory Coast's best performance was a 29-11 loss to Tonga, which rendered them unable to enter the quarter-finals round.

JAPAN

Rugby Union in Japan has a history stretching back to the later 19th century, when British sailors introduced the game to Yokohama and other ports. By the 1920s, Japan had nearly 60,000 rugby players registered across the country, and around 1500 clubs in operation. It wasn't until the early 1930s that Japan played their first international match – against Canada, who were also yet to play internationally. An Australian University side toured Japan next, but further interaction was impossible with the advent of war. Resourcefulness and speed are the hallmark of Japanese rugby, and from the post-war years onwards, the nation has continued to dominated the Asian rugby competition, and improve in the wider international arena.

Japan has played in every Rugby World Cup since 1987. Since their inaugural appearance, the *Cherry Blossoms* have improved against their competitors. Their 145-17 loss against New Zealand in 1995 was a low point, but since then their shrinking final score margins have indicated growing improvement.

Japan's highest try scorer in history is Daisuke Ohata, a wing and centre known for his speed. Ohata has 58 caps and 345 points to his name. Ohata is also the world's leading try scorer, with 69 tries from 58 matches in his career, and a single match tally of three tries against Georgia in 2006. Achilles tendon injuries, followed by a knee injury, forced his retirement in 2011.

The 2019 Rugby World Cup will be hosted by Japan, with Singapore and Hong Kong providing venues for ten of the matches. It will be the first time the tournament has been held in an Asian country.

1987

Japan failed to win any of its pool matches, but while the losses against England and Australia were fairly convincing, they nevertheless fought it out with the United States before losing 21-18.

1991
Japan managed a single but impressive 52-8 win over Zimbabwe in the pool stage, but losses to Ireland and Scotland saw them unable to continue into the knockout stage of the tournament.

1995
Pool stage matches against Wales and Ireland saw Japan lose, but not by the margins of earlier tournaments. Sadly, their 145-17 loss against New Zealand saw them dismissed from the tournament in their final match.

1999
Japan failed to win any of its pool stage matches in 1999, but they held their own in their 33-12 loss against Argentina.

2003
Japan might have lost all of its pool stage matches, but the losses were refreshingly smaller than in previous years. The margins were 21, 22, 28 and 13 points against Scotland, France, Fiji and the Unites States respectively, indicating promise for Japan in future tournaments.

2007
Japan performed well against Canada and Fiji, although they lost all four of their pool stage matches in 2007. Going down 91-3 to Australia and 72-18 to Wales, they were unable to proceed to the knockout quarter-finals round.

2011
A 23-23 draw with Canada was the high point of Japan's 2011 tournament. Although losses were scored in the three remaining matches of Japan's pool stage, the losing margins against two of the three teams showed that Japan was improving.

2015
Japan failed to get past the Pool stages at the 2015 World Cup losing to the United States 18-21, England 60-7 and Australia 42-23. As hosts for the 2019 event, Japan have spent the past four years creating a superior team that is sure to make a big impact.

NAMIBIA

Namibia first experienced rugby during World War I, when South African soldiers invaded and ousted German troops from the colony. Up until the time that Namibia won its independence, they played in South Africa's domestic Currie Cup competition. Finishing third in 1989, Namibia became an independent country the following year and formed its own Rugby Union before joining the International Rugby Board within a matter of weeks. Their former Currie Cup experience against South Africa proved to have been an excellent hardening process, and they found themselves beating Italy and Ireland the following year.

Known as the *Welwitschias*, Namibia went on to score victory in each of the 10 tests they played, downing such teams as Zimbabwe and Portugal. In their attempt to qualify for the 1995 Rugby World Cup, Namibia beat the Arabian Gulf, Zimbabwe and Kenya, but defeat at the hands of Ivory Coast and a draw with Morocco saw them bundled out of contention. In the African tournaments for 1999 qualification, Namibia finished second in Round 3 behind Zimbabwe. Having defeated Zimbabwe, the latter team won on points, but Namibia went on to defeat Ivory Coast, and Morocco, as well as winning again over Zimbabwe and losing to Tunisia before achieving qualification for the 1999 tournament. At one point, doubt over their inclusion arose when the government barred them from participating in a South African tournament – a strategy they had deployed to prepare themselves for the RWC. Eventually, they were allowed to participate, but in the years since the Currie Cup, Namibia had not flourished as a rugby nation, and the results bore this out.

Qualifying for 2003 and 2007, Namibia eventually won their fourth qualification in a row when they beat Ivory Coast and won a berth in the 2011 Rugby World Cup. The results of that tournament might not have spelled victory in terms of winning a single match, but the score margins were vastly improved – especially against Samoa and Fiji.

Notable Namibian players include Johnny Redelinghuys, a prop with 30 caps and five points to his name, along with Eugene Jantjies, a scrum-half with 36 caps, 33 points and a try. Full-back Chrysander Botha, who scored a try for Namibia in the 2011 Rugby World Cup, currently plays in the English Premiership for the Exeter Chiefs. Previously, Botha represented the Golden Lions in the Currie Cup, and in Super Rugby, he represented the Lions. He has 55 caps for Namibia and an impressive 215 points.

1999
Losses to Fiji, France and Canada saw Namibia dismissed from the cup at the pool stage.

2003
Falling 67-14 to Argentina in their first pool stage match, Namibia went on to lose 64-7 to Ireland and 142-0 to Australia (a current Rugby World Cup record). A final 37-7 loss to Romania saw Namibia exit the tournament.

2007
In 2007, Namibia lost 63-3 to Argentina, 87-10 to France, 30-0 to Georgia and 32-17 to Ireland in the pool stage matches. They were unable to advance to the knockout quarter-finals.

2011
Although Namibia failed to win a match in the pool stage of the 2011 tournament, the nation nevertheless fared moderately against Fiji and Samoa, indicating improvement. Unable to advance to the quarter-finals, Namibia exited the tournament scoreless.

2015
Namibia qualified for the 2015 tournament and was unlucky to be in the same group as New Zealand and Argentina. Massive defeats to New Zealand 58-14 and Argentina 64-19 saw the side fall to last in their group.

NEW ZEALAND

The number one ranked Rugby Union side in the world, and the current holders of the Webb Ellis Cup, is New Zealand. Since debuting internationally in 1903, the All Blacks have beaten every nation they have played at least once, and they have lost against only five of those teams in 112 years. Along with the Rugby World Cup, New Zealand also competes internationally in The Rugby Championship (formerly the Tri-Nations), the Bledisloe Cup, the Freedom Cup and various international tests against other nations. They have also held the number one position in the World Rugby Rankings longer than any of their rivals.

1987

As a co-host of the inaugural Rugby World Cup in 1987, New Zealand began in sizzling form to easily beat Italy, Fiji and Argentina and advance unbeaten into the quarter finals. In a tournament notorious for high winning margins, a 30-3 win over Scotland set them up for a semi-final and a 49-6 victory over Wales. New Zealand faced France in the final, and yet another wide margin saw the All Blacks take the Webb Ellis Cup 29-0 in front of delighted home crowd.

1991

New Zealand faced England on its rival's home soil for the first of the 1991 pool matches, winning 18-12 and advancing to the quarter-finals unbeaten. A 29-13 win over Canada set up a semi-final against traditional rivals, Australia. A loss to the Wallabies relegated New Zealand to face Scotland for the third place spot, which the All Blacks won convincingly.

1995

1995 saw New Zealand in South Africa, following a hiatus caused by the Apartheid-induced international sporting ban. Wins over Wales, Japan and Ireland took them to the quarter finals, where they beat Scotland convincingly to advance to face England in the semi-final. This time, New Zealand won, and advanced to the final to face South Africa. A close result saw South Africa the victors.

1999

Tonga, England and Italy fell early to New Zealand in the pool stage of the 1999 Rugby World Cup, hosted by Wales. Again, the All Blacks won their quarter-final easily against Scotland, but they fell 43-31 to France in the semi-final, and 22-18 to South Africa in the competition for third place.

2003

Back in the southern hemisphere in 2003, the Australia hosted tournament saw New Zealand continue its unbeaten pool stage record to play South Africa in the quarter-final. Taking the Springboks 29-9, they fell to Australia in the semi-final, but beat France to take third place.

2007

In France, New Zealand again reigned supreme against its pool rivals, leaving Scotland to lick its wounds after a 40-0 drubbing. For the first time in the cup's history, the All Blacks were knocked out in a quarter-final, falling to France in a closely contested, 20-18 match.

2011

Back on home turf for the 2011 Rugby World Cup, New Zealand were unstoppable in their pool matches, even managing to down France by a healthy 20 points. Plucky Argentina were no match for the All Blacks in the quarter-finals, and Australia fell on its sword 20-6 to see the All Blacks march into the final and face France. A tight 8-7 victory returned the Webb Ellis Cup to where it all began 24 years earlier.

2015

New Zealand breezed through their Pool matches defeating Argentina, Namibia, Georgia and Tonga before progressing to the Quarter finals where they thrashed France 62-13. The Semi Final proved to be difficult with New Zealand just getting through against South Africa 20-18. They met Australia in the final finally defeating them 32-17 at Twickenham Stadium, London in front of 80,000.

PORTUGAL

Portugal discovered the game of rugby around the same time that Spain did, and their first international was played against Spain in 1935. With the neighbouring Spanish Civil War in full swing, and the ensuing professional sports drought during World War II, it was not until the 1960s that Portugal was able to become serious about international rugby. In the late sixties, Portugal played Morocco, Belgium, Romania and Italy, faring well as an international *youngster*. Into the seventies and eighties, Portugal continued to improve, taking on the Netherlands, Czechoslovakia, Denmark, Morocco, Poland, Zimbabwe, Belgium and Italy, with winning streaks that indicated a rosy future for Portuguese rugby.

By the time the 1987 Rugby World Cup was mooted, Portugal was not a member nation of the IRB – as the inaugural tournament was by invitation only, Portugal missed out on being involved in a qualification process. For the 1991 Rugby World Cup qualification process, Portugal took on and beat Czechoslovakia, and advanced to the next round. There, they faced the Netherlands, but lost the match 32-3 and failed to qualify. For 1995, Portugal was again successful in their first qualifying round, losing only one of their three games. Facing Wales and Spain, they lost to each and were eliminated from the qualification process.

Not to be defeated, Portugal persisted with the 2003 Rugby World Cup qualifiers, but Spain and Poland proved too good for them, and they failed to advance. Finally, with the future of rugby in Portugal being nurtured by the IRB, the nation began the qualification process for the 2007 RWC. Wins over the Ukraine, Czech Republic, Georgia and Russia, they lost only to Romania in the *European Nations Cup Division 1*. A win against the Czech Republic, a draw with Russia and losses to Romania and Georgia resulted in Portugal advancing to Round 5, with a second in the pool and another step up the qualification ladder. Entering the *repechage* round after another pool second, Portugal was finally successful on aggregate points and qualified for the 2007 Rugby World Cup.

Although Portugal's 2007 performance resulted in straight losses in the pool stage rounds, they performed well for an inaugural competitor. Unlike many other teams in the tournament's history, *Os Lobos* scored in each of its four games, regardless of them ending in losses. Following the tournament, Portugal lost a number of its key, long term players, including Rui Corderio and Joaquim Ferreira. Their bid to qualify for the 2011 Rugby World Cup was hampered by a sudden dearth of experience, and they lost to Romania and Georgia and failed to achieve a footing in the *repechage* round. Portugal has also failed to qualify for the 2015 tournament.

Portugal's most capped player is Vasco Uva, with 96 caps, 13 tries and 65 points. Uva captained Portugal during the 2007 Rugby World Cup, although a fractured hand sidelined him for the final game against Romania. He was replaced as captain in 2008 by João Correia. Uva also played professionally for the French team, Montpellier Hérault, in 2007-08.

2007
Portugal lost all four of its pool stage matches in 2007, leaving the team unable to proceed to the quarter-finals knockout stage. Unlike Romania and Scotland, who competed in the same pool, Portugal scored points in each of its games.

ROMANIA

Outside of the European *Six Nations* tournament, Romania is considered by some as one of the strongest rugby sides on the continent. Known as *The Oaks,* Romania currently sit 18th in the World Rugby Rankings, and they are *European Nations Cup* competitors.

Rugby arrived in Romania with students returning from universities and colleges in France in the first 20 years of the last century. As one of the three teams competing in the 1924 Olympics, Romania took bronze, but apart from international games with the USA and France, rugby remained an esoteric game until after World War II. At that point, the communist regime took possession of Romanian rugby and used it, along with all other sports, as a propaganda tool against the Western World. The positive aspect of this stance was that Romanian rugby players became members of the armed forces and had every tool at their disposal to perfect their playing prowess on a full-time basis.

During the revolution in Romania, several rugby union players were killed, including the country's team captain, who was shot at a roadblock. As rugby became professional in the 1990s, Romanian rugby suffered a sudden decline, and it wasn't until the early 2000s that the nation began to climb out of the doldrums and take its place as a serious rugby force.

1987
Romania's inaugural Rugby World Cup pool match was against Zimbabwe, which they won in a closely fought 21-20 result. Subsequent losses against France and Scotland saw them unable to reach the quarter-finals.

1991
Although Romania lost 30-3 to France, their pool matches against Fiji and Canada ended in small winning margins. Romania did not advance to the quarter-finals.

1995
Romania's 1995 appearance saw them lose 34-3 to Canada, 21-8 to South Africa and 42-3 to Australia in the pool stage matches. They were unable to advance to the knock-out round.

1999
Losing 57-9 to Australia, Romania rebounded to take the United States by two points. A 30 point loss to Ireland sealed Romania's fate for 1999.

2003
Much like a number of competing nations not yet at a level commensurate with rugby's elite, Romania nevertheless fared well against Ireland before losing 45-17. A solid 37-7 victory over Namibia preceded 90-8 and 50-3 losses against Australia and Argentina respectively. With two wins under their belts, Romania edged closer to one day competing in the quarter-finals.

2007
A solitary 14-10 win over Portugal in the pool stage round curtailed Romania's hopes for 2007. Losing 0-42 to Scotland and 85-8 to New Zealand, a respectable 24-18 loss to Italy showed promise for 2011.

2011
The 2011 pool stage was unkind to Romania in 2011, but two of their matches ended with respectable losing margins. In the other two matches, a 43-8 loss to Argentina and a 67-3 drubbing by England left Romania still to reach a Rugby World Cup quarter-final.

2015
Despite some competitive games in their Pool, Romania failed to get past their first four games and finished 4th ahead of Canada.

RUSSIA

Russia did not accept their invitation to play in the 1987 inaugural Rugby World Cup, reputedly citing South Africa's membership of the International Rugby Board as the reason (South Africa was vetoed from international sporting competition at the time due to Apartheid). Russia did not enter the qualification process for 1991, but indicated interest for the ensuing four tournaments – failing to qualify each time. Eventually, Russia qualified for the 2011 tournament, but not for the 2015 Rugby World Cup.

Rugby was slow to reach Russia, and when it did, the country was governed by Stalin and was about to plunge headlong into World War II. Immediately after the war, Russia took great pains to separate itself from the rest of the world, and that separation included international sports. Eventually, when the Iron Curtain was at its strongest, it was mainly the Olympic Games that Russia used as a propaganda tool against life in the West – rugby barely received a mention. Eventually, Russia played its first international in the early 1970s, and by the 1980s they were regularly playing against Romania and Italy.

After the collapse of the Berlin Wall, some Russian rugby players were recruited into the *Commonwealth of Independent States* rugby team, but by 1992, Russia had its own national team and played in the *FIRA-AER European Trophy*. Since then, Russia has competed in the *European Nations Cup*, and has come close to taking the prize several times.

Russia declined an invitation to the 1987 Rugby World Cup, reportedly citing South Africa's involvement in the planning of the tournament as the reason – South Africa were still subject to an international sporting ban as a result of Apartheid. Russia did not enter the 1991 qualification process, but they began their bid to be involved in time for the 1995 tournament. Russia played in East Group A of the European qualifiers, winning both matches against Georgia and Poland to advance to Round 3. At that point, they beat Germany 69-5, but lost 30-0 to Romania and failed to qualify.

In the European qualification for 2003, Russia beat the Czech Republic 37-18 and dominated the Netherlands 65-3, eventually advancing to Round 5, where they beat Spain 36-6 and won a short-lived qualification. Once it was discovered that Russia had used South African players who were ineligible, they were expelled from the competition, and thus lost their right to compete in the 2003 tournament. Russia played in the *European Nations Cup Division 1* as part of their qualifying process for the 2007 Rugby World Cup. Winning on aggregate, they reached Round 5, but lost 67-7 to Italy and 26-23 to Portugal, bowing out of contention. As runner up of Division 1 in the *European Nations Cup*, Russia qualified for the 2011 tournament as the Europe 2 pick, with seven games won, one drawn and twp lost, trailing Georgia by two table points in the final tally.

Currently ranked 19th in the World Rugby Rankings, Russia is currently experiencing an influx of new players into its international side.

2011
Russia retired scoreless from the pool stage of the 2011 tournament, losing 13-6 to the United States, 53-17 to Italy, 62-12 to Ireland and 68-22 to Australia.

SAMOA

Ranked seventeenth in world rugby, Samoa initially entered the Rugby World Cup in 1991 as Western Samoa. Now known as *Manu Samoa*, the island nation has played rugby since the game first arrived with Catholic missionaries in the 1920s. Within a few years, Western Samoa, Tonga and Fiji formed a regular competition, touring the pacific to play against each other. With New Zealand their ultimate goal, Western Samoa eventually toured New Zealand in the 1970s, and a visit by Wales in the early 1980s resulted in Western Samoa visiting Wales and achieving international recognition.

Much to the surprise of many in international rugby circles, Western Samoa was not invited to play in the 1987 Rugby World Cup, but a subsequent European tour led to participation in the Tokyo elimination series and a berth in the 1991 Rugby World Cup. The tiny island nation advanced to the quarter-finals in their debut, leaving nobody in any doubt as to their future in international competition. Many notable All Blacks players originate from Samoa, and alternatively, a number of Manu Samoa players are New Zealand born – this has led to complications for players on both sides wishing to represent their nation of birth in World Cup Rugby.

Since 1997, the team has been known as Samoa, or *Manu Samoa*. With most of the team devout Christians, they do not play or train on Sundays. Manu Samoa has reached the Rugby World Cup quarter-finals twice, and the quarter-final play-offs once in the history of the tournament.

1991
Western Samoa's first year saw them beat Wales in the tournament's biggest upset, before losing to Australia and defeating Argentina. They advanced to the quarter-finals to face Scotland, who won convincingly and bundled the newcomers out of the tournament.

1995
A single loss to England in the pool stage round saw Western Samoa advance to the quarter-finals. Facing the Springboks, they were bundled 42-14 out of cup contention.

1999
Samoa gave Japan a 43-9 hiding in the first match of the pool stage, but they fell against a nascent Argentina in their next match. A victory against Wales buoyed the spirits and sent Samoa to the newly introduced quarter-final play-offs. They fell 35-20 to Scotland and were unable to proceed to the quarter-finals.

2003
In a first match that saw a 60-13 drubbing of Uruguay, Samoa then took on Georgia to win 46-9. South Africa and England proved too tough a nut to crack for Samoa, but their loss margins were not enormous, and they retired respectably from the 2003 tournament.

2007
Losing to South Africa by a large margin, Samoa held its own against England and Tonga, losing both matches by a moderate number of points. Victory came against the Unites States in a close match, but it was not enough to see Samoa advance to the quarter-finals.

2011
A 49-12 win over Namibia and a 27-7 victory against Fiji were not enough for Samoa to advance to the quarter-finals. Losing 17-10 to Wales and 13-5 to South Africa, Samoa ended its bid for the 2011 Rugby World Cup.

2015
Samoa started the 2015 tournament with a 25-16 win against the United States but then lost their next three games to South Africa 46-6, Japan 26-5 and Scotland 36-33. The team captured the hearts of the rugby public during the tournament and showed massive promise for 2019.

SCOTLAND

Scotland is ranked seventh in the World Rugby Rankings, and their rugby pedigree extends back to the early 1870s, when they challenged England to a match that ultimately became their first international game in Edinburgh, and which led to the *Calcutta Cup* in 1878 and continuing rivalry between both nations for it since. With a hiatus during the war years throughout the first half of the 20th century, Scotland finally dipped its toe back in the waters of rugby in the early 1950s. It was not until the 1960s that Scotland led the way and began a nationwide league for the game, at which point professionalism entered the sport. In the early 2000s, Scotland took a dive internationally, and in the ensuing 15 years, their form has had a chequered history of lows and highs. Scotland's greatest strength is the ability to surprise the opposition, and it is that quality that keeps fans on the edges of their seats until the final whistle.

The home of Scottish Rugby Union is Murrayfield Stadium, built in 1925 and used as an Army supply depot during World War II. Over the years, the stadium has been renovated accommodate a growing international spectator audience, and it hosted matches during the 2007 Rugby World Cup with a seating capacity of over 100,000.

1987
After a surprise draw with France in the first of their pool matches in 1987, Scotland went on to beat Zimbabwe and Romania and advance to the knockout quarter-finals. The unstoppable All Blacks saw Scotland bundled out in a 30-3 loss.

1991
Faring well in the pool stage, Scotland beat Japan, Zimbabwe and Ireland to advance undefeated to the knockout round. There, they won convincingly over Western Samoa and faced England in the semi-final. A low scoring 9-6 loss resulted in a battle for third place against the All Blacks, with New Zealand winning 13-6.

1995
Scoring an early 89-0 victory over Ivory Coast, Scotland gave Tonga a 41-5 pasting before France held them to account with a sobering 22-19 result. The quarter-finals saw Scotland face New Zealand, who won 48-30.

1999
Scotland lost early to South Africa, but beat Uruguay and Spain to win a berth in the newly introduced quarter-final play-offs. A 35-20 win over Samoa saw Scotland face New Zealand in the quarter-finals, but they were dismissed from the tournament after losing 30-8.

2003
Losing only one of their pool stage matches, Scotland advanced to the quarter-finals confidently. A 33-16 loss to the Wallabies saw them knocked out of the tournament.

2007
Losing only one of their four pool stage matches in a 40-0 massacre, Scotland nevertheless outperformed Italy, Portugal and Romania to advance to the quarter-finals. Argentina, in its best year yet, dismissed Scotland 19-13 from the tournament.

2011
It was Argentina's growing strength that bundled Scotland out of quarter-finals contention for 2011, with a 13-12 result. Losing 16-12 to England saw Scotland third in the pool, with no chance of remaining in the tournament.

2015
Scotland lost to Australia by a single point in the Quarter Final of the 2015 World Cup 35-34 but had a promising tournament with wins over Romania and Georgia - losing narrowly to England 16-12 and Argentina 13-12 in Pool B.

SOUTH AFRICA

While South Africa was involved in creating the Rugby World Cup, an international sporting ban rendered them unable to compete until talks to end Apartheid in their country began. By that time, the 1995 tournament loomed, and South Africa won the bid to host it.

Ranked fifth in the World Rugby Rankings, the Springboks have a rugby pedigree that stretches back over 125 years. The division of races had always interfered with South Africa's game, reducing competition on home soil to 'Whites Only' and exposing players to international criticism for their government's stance whenever they toured. Since the abolition of Apartheid, South Africa currently competes in The Rugby Championship (formerly known as the Tri-Nations), the Freedom Cup and the Mandela Plate Challenge, as well as a number of Tests against various nations. South Africa's victory in its debut Rugby World Cup was not just a win for their nation on home soil – it proved that sport has the ability to tear down walls and triumph over discrimination.

1995
The Springbok's debut into the Rugby World Cup began with a 28-18 win over Australia in front of a home crowd. Wins against Romania and Canada saw them advance unbeaten to face Western Samoa in the quarter-finals. A 42-14 victory saw France and South Africa fight it out in a hard contest that the Springboks finally won. Facing their toughest competitor in the final, the Springboks emerged victorious with a 15-12 win over the All Blacks.

1999
South Africa played all of its pool matches in Edinburgh in 1999, advancing unbeaten into the quarter-finals. In a year that saw newly introduced play-offs for some teams vying for quarter-finals spots, the Springboks earned a week's rest before facing England. A 44-21 win over the tournament's co-hosts resulted in an Australia-South Africa match in the semi-finals. Australia won 27-21, leaving the Springboks to triumph over New Zealand in the battle for third place.

2003
For the first time since entering the Rugby World Cup tournament, South Africa suffered a single defeat against England, but the Springboks nevertheless advanced into the quarter-finals. Again facing their toughest rivals, New Zealand triumphed 29-9 on the day, and South Africa was knocked out – the first time they didn't make the semi-finals since first entering the competition.

2007
A reinvigorated South Africa set off in style to take all of its pool matches in 2007 and advance unbeaten in to the quarter-finals. A 37-20 win over Fiji saw the Springboks facing, and beating, Argentina in the semi-finals, which led to a face-off with England for the cup. For the second time in 12 years, the Springboks emerged victorious as the victors of the Webb Ellis Cup.

2011
Unlike most of their rivals, the Springboks had not yet played World Cup Rugby in New Zealand, and after a single-point win over Wales, they again bulldozed their way through the pool stage and into the quarter-finals. Perhaps in the biggest upset yet, South Africa fell to Australia and were bundled out of the tournament before the semi-finals.

2015
The highly contested match between Japan and South Africa in the opening weekend, which Japan scored the winning try in the added minutes over heavily favoured South Africa, was widely considered as the "biggest upset" in the history of rugby. As a result, much media attention was drawn right from the beginning of this tournament. South Africa narrowly lost to New Zealand in the knockout stage but finished third defeating Argentina 24-13. In the Quarter Finals, South Africa narrowly won against Wales 23-19 at Twickenham but New Zealand awaited them in the Semi Finals.

SPAIN

Spain, or *Los Leones* have played in only one Rugby World Cup, but the game's history on the Iberian Peninsula began before World War I, when French and British exiles played in Barcelona. Beating Italy in their first official international, Spain spent the 1930s playing other European nations and generally winning. The Spanish Civil War and World War II interrupted rugby at that point (although Spain were neutral during the latter, most European nations were at war), and it wasn't until the 1950s that the game began again, but with lacklustre results. In the later 1960s, Spain again came into its own, beating such nations as Poland, the Netherlands, Morocco, Romania and Portugal and slowly garnering international strength and respect.

Not yet ready to take part in the global competition, Spain nevertheless strove to qualify for the Rugby World Cup, and in 1999, they finally saw their dream realised after a torrid qualification process. In the European qualification's Pool 3, Round B, they won each of their four games and managed to trump Portugal, who joined them with Scotland in the next pool round. Spain came second, and won their qualification to the 1999 tournament. Spain again beat Portugal in the qualifying process for the 2003 tournament, but after losses to Romania and Italy, they were up against Russia in the *repechage* round. After a win over Tunisia, it was the United States who stopped Spain from qualifying. A resurgent Spain began their road to 2007 qualification at top of Round 2 in the European qualification, advancing to Round 3 to win all four of those matches. Initially losing to Germany, they took the second match and continued on to Round 4 and victory over the Czech Republic. Finally, their journey unravelled in Round 5 at the hands of Georgia and Romania. Qualification for 2011 was also unsuccessful.

In 2014, there were over 50,000 registered rugby players belonging to 221 Spanish clubs. Geographically, rugby continues to expand in Spain, and its popularity took a leap after the 1999 cup, regardless of their try-less tournament.

One of Spain's most notable rugby players is Alberto Malo, who still rates as one of the country's best ever players 20 years after his retirement. Malo captained Spain in the 1999 Rugby World Cup and holds 89 caps, with a point score of 26. Fullback and flyhalf Francisco Puertas Soto also played in the 1999 team, and he held 93 caps when he retired in 2001. One of today's Spanish rugby heroes is César Sempere, who plays wing, fly half and fullback, and has 53 caps and 31 international tries to his name. Other notable Spanish rugby players have played overseas, including Oriol Ripol, who has played for the Rotherhampton Tiitans and the Northampton Saints in England, and spent seven seasons in the United Kingdom. Cédric Garcia is another, having played for French teams Montauban, Bayonne and Castres as a scrum-half, as well as representing Spain in 2004.

1999

A disappointing 27-15 loss against Uruguay was the first of Spain's three pool stage match losses in 1999. Further losses to South Africa (47-3) and Scotland (48-0) heralded their departure from the last Rugby World Cup of the 20th century.

TONGA

Missionaries and sailors introduced rugby to Tonga in the early 20th century, and since then, the Pacific nation has taken to the sport with a trademark fierceness that often leaves opponents wondering what hit them. Apart from short tours of New Zealand, Australia and Great Britain, Tonga were relatively unknown in international rugby circles until the mid 1980s, preferring instead to involve themselves in their Pacific tournaments against Fiji and Samoa. Apart from 1991, Tonga has played in every Rugby World Cup, and it was in 1995 that a match against Ivory Coast resulted in their opponent's winger, Max Brito, sustaining an injury that left him permanently and tragically paralysed.

Tonga's fortunes have ebbed and flowed in international rugby, and after failing to make the 1991 tournament, a 1994 South Pacific championship win helped them ultimately qualify on points difference for 1995. Tonga's greatest rugby victory has not been in the Rugby World Cup, but beating the French touring team 20-16 buoyed the nation's spirits in 1999. A further Rugby World Cup win over the French in the 2011 tournament pool stage matches has given rise to speculation about Tonga's fortunes for 2015. They currently sit 13th in the World Rugby Rankings.

One of Tonga's most prolific and well known players is Nili Latu, who at 33 years old debuted internationally for Tonga in 2006. Latu was a talented tackler, and was included in the Independent Newspaper's list of the 50 best world rugby players in 2008.

1987
Tonga's entry into the inaugural Rugby World Cup was short lived, losing 37-4 to Canada and 32-9 to Ireland. Their 29-16 loss to Wales ended their dream of advancing, but was a respectable score nevertheless.

1991
Tonga failed to qualify for the 1991 Rugby World Cup

1995
Tonga lost 38-10 to France in the first of its pool stage matches, and was downed 41-5 by Scotland next. A 29-11 victory over Ivory Coast was not enough to score a berth in the quarter-finals.

1999
Losing 45-9 to New Zealand, Tonga rebounded to take the Italy match 28-25. Sadly, a 101-10 drubbing by England dampened the spirits and left Tonga without the opportunity to advance.

2003
2003 was not the best Rugby World Cup year for Tonga, who lost 36-12 to Italy, 27-20 to Wales, 91-7 to New Zealand and 24-7 to Canada. They were unable to advance to the quarter-finals.

2007
Tonga beat the United States and Samoa in closely contested games in the pool stage matches. A 30-25 loss against South Africa and a further 36-20 loss to England cut short Tonga's hopes for quarter-finals contention.

2011
Pipped by France on points for a berth in the quarter-finals, Tonga came close in 2011. Losing 41-10 to New Zealand and 25-20 to Canada, Tonga then scored a 31-18 victory over Japan and a surprising 19-14 win against France, who nevertheless beat Tonga on points to advance.

2015
Winning only 1 game in their Pool (35-21 Namibia), Tonga faced tough opposition at the tournament in their group including New Zealand and Argentina.

UNITED STATES

It was on the west coast of the United States that rugby first became popular, although its offshoot, American Football, has always taken precedence. Beginning with a USA/Canada international when Harvard University played McGill University in the mid 1870s, rugby found its way to California, and an international team played both Australia and New Zealand before the nation's involvement in World War I brought it to a halt. At that time, rugby was considered a far safer sport than American Football, the latter of which was almost outlawed by the country's President as a result of the thuggery and deaths it caused.

The USA's first foray into international rugby outside of its borders was for the 1920 Olympics, where only two teams competed – the United States and the much stronger France. Surprisingly, the United States took gold in the 1920 Olympics, and they again bested France to emerge victorious at the 1924 Olympics. At that time in the USA, American Football had been cleaned up, and was on what would eventuate in a meteoric rise in popularity – leaving rugby in the USA a much poorer cousin from that time on.

Struggling through the 1960s and 1970s, but with several notable wins in the 1980s, the USA were finally on the path to the inaugural Rugby World Cup. Known as the *Eagles*, they have only missed qualifying for the tournament once. The United States is currently ranked 15th in the World Rugby Rankings.

1987
Up against Australia and England in its pool matches, the United States was not in contention for the inaugural quarter-finals, but a 21-18 win over Japan saw them take home a single victory in the ultimate rugby competition.

1991
Losses to New Zealand, England and Italy saw the United States knocked out of the 1991 tournament in the pool stage.

1995
The United States did not qualify for the 1995 Rugby World Cup.

1999
After missing out in 1995, the United States played their first Rugby World Cup pool match after eight years - losing 53-8 to Ireland on Irish home soil. Their next match was a closely contested one against Romania, resulting in a mere two-point loss, but a 55-19 score at the hands of the Wallabies ended American dreams for another tournament.

2003
Although they scored a win against Japan in the pool stage, the United States lost to Fiji by a single point, and then by respectable margins to France and Scotland – a sign of a team ready to rise in the ranks of world rugby, and one to watch in future tournaments.

2007
Losses to England, Samoa, South Africa and Tonga in the pool stage round curtailed any hope of reaching quarter-finals contention. Interestingly, the final scores against all but South Africa were more than respectable and showed promise for the United States.

2011
An initial 22-10 loss to Ireland preceded a 13-6 victory over Russia in 2011. Losing 67-5 to Australia and 27-10 to Italy ended the United States' dreams of quarter-finals contention in 2011.

2015
Losses to Samoa, Scotland, South Africa and Japan in the Pool matches, saw the United States out of the 2015 tournament.The most telling defeat was against South Africa - 64-0.

URUGUAY

Known as the *Teros*, Uruguay first qualified for the Rugby World Cup in 1999, and again for the 2003 tournament. The country's international rugby history began in the late 1940s with involvement in the *Pan American Games*, and later the *South American Rugby Championship* of the 1950s. Playing against Chile, Argentina, Montevideo and Brazil among others, Uruguay set out to reach the pinnacle of South American and International rugby.

In the 1970s, the number of matches won began to outweigh losses, and by the 1980s, Uruguay experienced winning streaks lasting several years at a time in the South American competition. With Argentina still dominating the competition over-all, Uruguay was unable to qualify for the Rugby World Cup until 1999, when they scored a win against Spain and finished third in the pool stage of the tournament. As winners of the 2009 *South American Rugby Championship-A*, and the 2013 *South American Rugby Championship-A*, Uruguay's growing rugby prowess took it to the *repechage* round to qualify for the 2015 Rugby World Cup.

Among Uruguay's most notable players is Diego Aguirre, a fly-half with 74 caps and 154 aggregate points. During his career, which spanned 1995 to 2007, Aguirre scored 26 penalties, 17 conversions and 11 tries. He played at the 1999 and 2003 Rugby World Cups, captaining the 2003 side. Diego Ormaechea, a former player and now a professional coach, played for Uruguay from 1979 to 1999, with 73 caps. In his 20 year international career, Ormaechea scored 16 tries, and he was the oldest player in Rugby World Cup history, captaining Uruguay at the age of 40. Uruguay's current captain is Nicolás Klappenbach, a hooker with 38 caps. Klappenbach played in the unsuccessful qualifying squads for the 2007 and 2011 tournaments.

1999
Uruguay took an initial 27-15 win over Spain in their first pool stage match, but fell 43-12 to Scotland and 39-3 to South Africa. Unable to advance to the quarter-final play-offs, they at least took home one convincing win.

2003
Uruguay fell early and in spectacular fashion 72-6 to South Africa, and again in a 60-13 loss to Samoa. Taking on Georgia, they emerged victorious with a 24-12 win, before falling 111-13 to England and bowing out of the tournament.

2007
Uruguay did not qualify for the 2007 Rugby World Cup.

2011
Uruguay did not qualify for the 2011 Rugby World Cup.

2015
Uruguay qualified for the 2015 Rugby World Cup by defeating Russia by an aggregate score of 57–49 in the two-game series, winning the second game at home 36–27 in front of 14,000 fans at the Charrua Stadium. With 4 massive losses against Wales, Australia, Fiji and England, Uruguay bowed out of the 2015 Cup.

WALES

Wales' rugby pedigree goes back to the mid 19th century when the game was introduced into schools. Within 30 years, Wales was at the forefront of the game, devising a new formation that increased the game's back by one player, and decreased the forward players by one. This formation went on to be adopted internationally. Fro that time on Wales' winning record was formidable, and apart from a post WWI slump during the depression, the nation continued on into the 1950s as a dominant rugby force.

By the time of the inaugural Rugby World Cup, Wales' rugby record was in a state of decline, but as a new century dawned, so did a resurgent Wales. Their recent performance in the Northern Hemisphere's *Six Nations Championship* indicates that the Welsh are again a dominant rugby force, and they currently sit second in the World Rugby Rankings.

1987
Wales bulldozed Ireland, Tonga and Canada to reach the quarter-finals unbeaten in 1987. Their winning streak continued in a 16-3 victory over England, but it was the All Blacks who stopped them short in a disappointing, 49-6 semi-final result. The battle for third place saw Wales face and defeat the Wallabies in a hard fought 22-21 match.

1991
In a surprise upset, Wales' firs pool match saw them lose to newcomers Wester Samoa in a 61-13 result. A 16-7 victory over Argentina was not enough to soften the blow of a 38-3 thumping by the Wallabies, and Wales failed to advance into the quarter-finals.

1995
A 57-10 victory over Japan was not enough to see Wales advance to the knock-out round in 1995. A 34-9 loss against New Zealand preceded a nail-biting 24-23 defeat at the hands of Ireland and the end of the 1995 Rugby World Cup for the Welsh.

1999
The fourth Rugby World Cup saw Wales defeat Argentina 23-18 in the first of its pool stage matches, and trounce Japan 64-15 next. It was Samoa who gave the Welsh an upset, winning 39-31, but Wales nevertheless advanced to the quarter-final without having to take part in the newly introduced play-offs. A 24-9 loss to Australia saw Wales retire from the tournament.

2003
With the increased number of teams in the pools stage in 2003, Wales beat Canada, Tonga and Italy convincingly, before losing 53-37 to the All Blacks. Nevertheless, Wales advanced to the quarter-finals, where they were bundled out of the tournament in a 28-17 loss to England.

2007
2007 was Wales' Rugby World Cup *annus horribilis*. Of the four pool stage matches, Wales won only two, going down 32-20 to Australia and 38-34 to Fiji. They were unable to advance to the quarter-finals, one of which was held in Cardiff.

2011
With only a single point loss to South Africa in the first of the pool stage matches, Wales went on to win the remaining three games against Samoa, Namibia and Fiji. Advancing to the quarter-finals, they beat Ireland 22-10 and faced France in the semi-finals. In what proved to be a low-scoring game, Wales fell 9-8 and played Australia for bronze. Losing 21-18, Wales again failed to take home a trophy.

2015
At the 2015 World Cup Wales were in the same pool as Australia, England, Fiji and Uruguay. They finished second in the pool behind Australia and ahead of hosts England. South Africa defeated Wales in the quarter final.

ZIMBABWE

Rugby arrived in Zimbabwe in 1890 when it was known as Rhodesia. Within five years, the Rhodesia Rugby Football Union came into existence, giving Zimbabwe a rugby heritage equivalent to many European countries. Before the 19th century was over, Rhodesia had toured South Africa with a team comprised of the best players from the nation's five major clubs. In the first 20 years of the next century, British teams were touring, and by 1930, New Zealand had also visited. When the British toured South Africa in 1938, they visited Rhodesia, winning both matches, but in 1949, the All Blacks finally fell victim 10-8 and gave the country its first international victory of note. From that point on, the nation came into its own as a rugby contender, reaching its peak in the 1970s. A reasonable number of players were so good that they were selected to play for South Africa.

When Zimbabwe became an independent nation in 1980, their national rugby team immediately toured England. They played their first official international against Kenya the following year, winning 34-24 and leaving nobody in any doubt that they were an African side well able to compete at an international level. Their invitation to compete in the inaugural Rugby World Cup in 1987 was thus not a great surprise to those following rugby on the African continent.

Zimbabwe as a nation was not without its economic worries, and a drop in living standards affected everything – including sports. This reduced the funds and facilities available for rugby in Zimbabwe beyond secondary schooling, and had a major effect on the nation's elite. Many of Zimbabwe's elite players departed for South Africa, Australia, New Zealand and Europe, with lucrative, professional salaries too enticing to ignore. Today, upcoming young talents have continued to leave Zimbabwe to further their professional careers, leaving the state of the nation's rugby culture in the doldrums.

Zimbabwean rugby greats who have departed include Tendai Mtawarira, who was spotted by coach Joey Muwadzuri. Winger Takudzwa Ngwenya was first offered a place in the English *Guinness Premiership*, but instead moved to play for the French club *Biarritz Olympique*. Since 2007, he has represented the United States in the Rugby World Cup.

Zimbabwe has failed to qualify for the Rugby World Cup since its last appearance in 1991. For the 2015 tournament, Zimbabwe's attempt to qualify reached the *repechage* round, but they were defeated 23-15 by Russia in the semi-final.

1987
Zimbabwe lost 21-20 to Romania and 60-21 to Scotland in the pool stage. A 70-12 defeat at the hands of France saw Zimbabwe unable to proceed to the quarter-finals.

1991
Losing 55-11 to Ireland and 51-12 to Scotland, Zimbabwe faced Japan to lose in a 52-8 drubbing in Belfast, Ireland. They were unable to proceed to the quarter-finals.

MEMORABLE MOMENTS

Australia humiliate Namibia – RWC 2003

Australia broke the record for the largest margin of victory in a World Cup by beating Namibia 142-0 in a game that emphasised the gulf in class between the top teams and those lower down the rankings. The Aussies opened the scoring after just two minutes, and didn't really stop after that, racking up an unbelievable 22 tries during the course of the game.

MEMORABLE MOMENTS

Western Samoa shock Wales – RWC 1991

Wales, and the rest of the world of rugby, were stunned when massive underdogs Western Samoa pulled off a shock victory over the Welsh in the group stages of the 1991 tournament, coming out on top in a closely contested match that ended 16-13. Wales were playing at home and expected to win easily, but the Samoans had different ideas.

MEMORABLE MOMENTS

John Kirwan's solo try – RWC 1987

In the first ever Rugby World Cup match, hosts New Zealand demolished Italy with a convincing 70-6 win. The highlight of the match was John Kirwan's solo try, in which he rounded half of the opposition team after receiving the ball deep in his own half. Still regarded as one of the greatest tries the tournament has ever seen, Kirwan's pace and agility were far too much for the Italians, most of whom weren't able to lay a finger on him.

MEMORABLE MOMENTS

Haka vs. Sipi Tau – RWC 2011

The 2011 Rugby World Cup was started in style when New Zealand and Tonga faced off against each other with their pre-match rituals, the Haka and the Sipi Tau. By the time both teams had finished their traditional war dances, it's safe to say not a single person in the stadium didn't have goosebumps.

MEMORABLE MOMENTS

Jonny Wilkinson kicks a last minute winner – RWC 2003

Jonny Wilkinson won the game in the 2003 final with a late kick taken on his weaker right foot. There were only 20 seconds left on the clock, and it was enough for England to win their first ever Rugby World Cup, with a narrow victory of 20-17. Simply an unforgettable moment for English rugby fans and one that the Wallabies would like to forget.

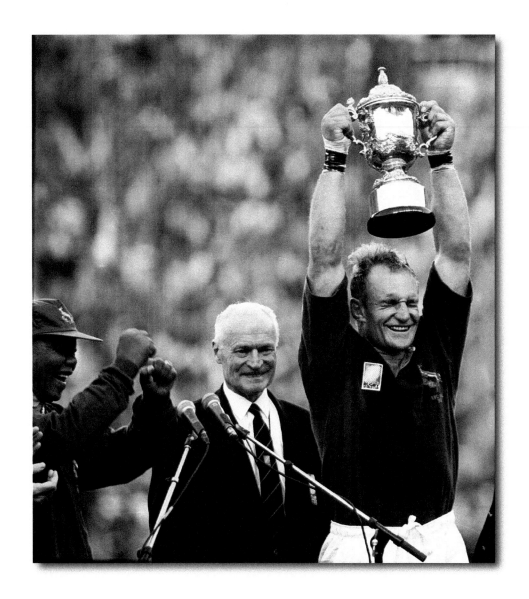

MEMORABLE MOMENTS

Mandela hands Pienaar the trophy – RWC 1995

The truly remarkable tale of rugby uniting a racially divided country reached its pinnacle when South Africa beat New Zealand 15-12 in a closely fought final in 1995. Nelson Mandela in his Springboks jersey presenting the trophy to captain Francois Pienaar perfectly symbolised the 'Rainbow Nation' that the country had become.

MEMORABLE MOMENTS

Stephen Larkham picks a good time for his first drop goal – RWC 1999

A close fought semi-final between Australia and South Africa in the 1999 tournament was taken to extra time by renowned Springboks kicker Jannie de Beer. However, it was a kick by Aussie fly-half Stephen Larkham that stole the headlines, winning the game in the dying moments. As if that wasn't enough, it was Larkham's first ever international drop goal, he scored it from 50 metres (54 yards) out, and he had an injured knee – talk about working well under pressure.

MEMORABLE MOMENTS

Ngwenya leaves Habana for dead – RWC 2007

In one of the tries of the tournament, the USA's Takudzwa Ngwenya rocketed past supposed fastest player in the world Bryan Habana, much to the shock of the South African. It wasn't enough to prevent a victory for the Springboks but provided the 2007 World Cup with one of its most memorable moments.

MEMORABLE MOMENTS

Les Bleus fight back against New Zealand – RWC 1999

When tournament favorites New Zealand went up against France in the 1999 semi-final, everybody expected a routine victory for the Johah Lomu inspired All Blacks. Things seemed to be going to plan when New Zealand found themselves with an early 24-10 lead, but France clearly hadn't read the script, dismantling the favorites by scoring 33 points without reply. Jeff Wilson managed to score a consolation try, but it wasn't enough to prevent one of the greatest upsets in Rugby World Cup history, with France winning 43-31.

MEMORABLE MOMENTS

Jonah Lomu steamrolls England – RWC 1995

Man-mountain Jonah Lomu burst onto the scene in the 1995 World Cup with an unstoppable performance against England in the semi-final. At 6ft 5in and 19 stone the young New Zealander pulverised the English defense, running through them like they weren't even there. Mike Catt will be testament to this, as he was flattened in the wake of Lomu scoring the first of his four tries in the game.

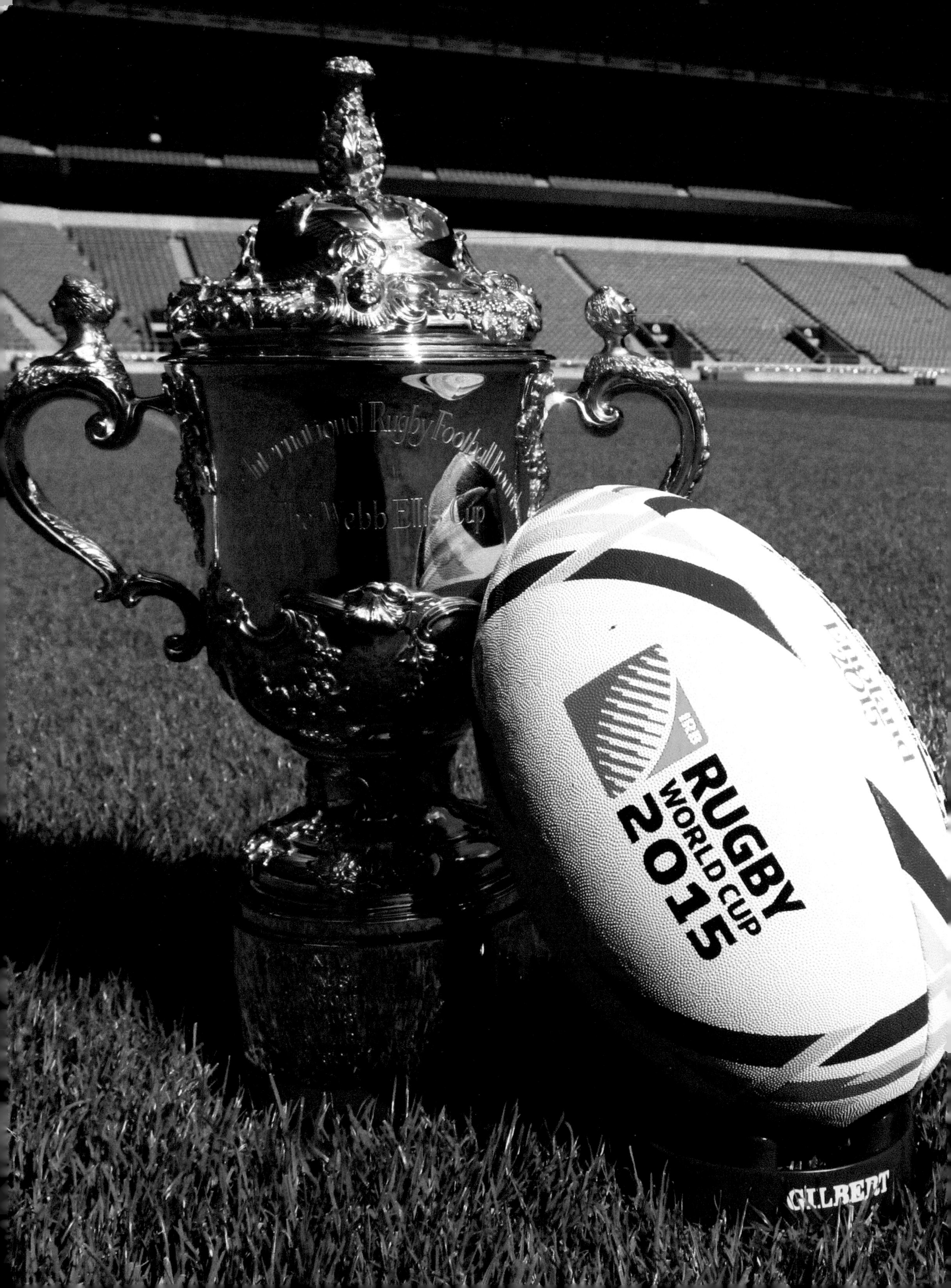
RUGBY
WORLD CUP
2015
GILBERT